Architecture That Speaks

Centennial Series of the Association of Former Students
Texas A&M University

Publication of this book was generously supported by

W. Lewis Barlow IV '70, FAIA, FAPT
in appreciation of the College of Architecture at Texas A&M University and its professors

Stephen H. '82 and Lisa Lucy
in celebration of the architectural heritage of Texas A&M University

Janet Howe '71
in honor of dear friends David G. Woodcock and Nancy T. McCoy

Architecture That Speaks

S. C. P. Vosper and Ten Remarkable Buildings at Texas A&M

Nancy T. McCoy and David G. Woodcock

Photographs by Carolyn Brown

Foreword by Michael K. Young

TEXAS A&M UNIVERSITY PRESS / COLLEGE STATION

This paper meets the requirements
of ANSI/NISO Z39.48–1992 (Permanence of Paper).
Binding materials have been chosen for durability.
Manufactured in China by Everbest Printing Co.
through FCI Print Group

Library of Congress Cataloging-in-Publication Data

Names: McCoy, Nancy T., 1959– author. | Woodcock, David G., 1937– author. | Brown, Carolyn, 1936– photographer.
Title: Architecture that speaks : S.C.P. Vosper and ten remarkable buildings at Texas A&M / Nancy T. McCoy and David G. Woodcock ;
    photographs by Carolyn Brown.
Other titles: Centennial series of the Association of Former Students, Texas A&M University ; no. 127.
Description: First edition. | College Station : Texas A&M University Press, [2017] | Series: Centennial series of the Association of Former
    Students, Texas A&M University ; number 127 | Includes bibliographical references and index.
Identifiers: LCCN 2017010414| ISBN 9781623495534 (book/cloth : alk. paper) | ISBN 9781623495541 (ebook)
Subjects: LCSH: Texas A & M University—Buildings—Designs and plans. | College buildings—Texas—College Station—Designs and plans. |
    College Station (Tex.)—Buildings, structures, etc. | Architecture—Conservation and restoration—Texas—College Station. | Vosper, S. C. P.,
    1887-1958.
Classification: LCC LD5309 .M33 2017 | DDC 378.764/242—dc23 LC record available at https://lccn.loc.gov/2017010414

Contents

Foreword

THE AUTHORS of this exceptional book have noted that Winston Churchill once famously said, "We shape our buildings, and afterwards our buildings shape us."

As a university president, I have had many occasions to reflect on the truth of Churchill's premise. Great universities require great buildings. They need spaces that lend themselves to discourse and inquiry, to research and debate, and to quiet reflection and thoughtful attention to the reflections of others.

With illuminating words and rich images, Nancy McCoy, David Woodcock, and Carolyn Brown introduce us to the architect Samuel Charles Phelps Vosper, who with the cooperation and guidance of Frederick E. Giesecke envisioned and designed some of the most aesthetically pleasing, well-used, and deeply admired buildings on the campus of Texas A&M University—or the Agricultural and Mechanical College of Texas, as it was then known. Starting in 1929, under the direction of Giesecke as college architect, Vosper designed ten buildings that would become the most significant structures on the campus at that time. In the decades since, these structures have, in many ways, remained closely connected to the historic heart and soul of Texas A&M University.

Anyone who has been stirred by the classic elegance of the front façade of the Jack K. Williams Administration Building, or who has admired the meticulous grace of the adornments on the interior of Cushing Library, or even who, perhaps in a moment of lapsed attention during a lecture, has stared in fascination at the geometric perfection of the stained-glass windows in Halbouty Auditorium has been impacted by the design genius of S. C. P. Vosper. As the authors make clear, Vosper, in giving shape to these iconic buildings, also gave shape to the students, faculty, staff—and, indeed, the history—of this great university. His is a heritage of beauty and utility that is well worth celebrating.

I commend this book to you, a thoughtful tribute to an architectural and aesthetic legacy that remains intimately linked with the importance of place for all Aggies, as well as the proud character and tradition of Texas A&M University.

—Michael K. Young
President, Texas A&M University
January 2017

Preface

WE ARE surrounded by buildings, we spend our lives in buildings, and we generally take them for granted, at least so long as they meet our basic functional needs. Buildings are recognized as landmarks for navigation and are often used as symbols to identify a specific location, and in those cases we "see" them as more than bricks and mortar, but we rarely stop to consider what makes them unique or special. A photographer with an ability to "see" draws our attention to the qualities, sometimes intangible, that make architecture an important part of our environment.

Carolyn Brown is one of those photographers. She has worked across the globe and is as fascinated with the swamps of Caddo Lake as she is with Egyptian temples. She came to the Texas A&M University campus in 2014 to spend one day documenting ten buildings for a lecture to be given by Nancy McCoy and Justin Curtsinger. Carolyn became enchanted with these buildings and during the course of the next two years visited many more times to photograph them with the intention of creating a book. All photographs throughout this book are by Carolyn Brown, unless otherwise noted.

Nancy McCoy, the preservation architect who commissioned the original photography, developed a deep appreciation for the buildings while providing architectural services for the Jack K. Williams Building and Scoates Hall. At Scoates, she found a department head with an unexpected passion for the building, which led her to seek a grant from the Cynthia Woods Mitchell Fund for Historic Interiors administered by the National Trust for Historic Preservation. The grant supported an investigation of the decoration in one of the ten buildings of the Depression Era designed by Samuel Charles Phelps (S. C. P.) Vosper.

David Woodcock left his native England and arrived on the campus when Vosper's buildings were only about thirty years old. With nearly fifty years teaching architecture, and using the campus as a living classroom, he would be instrumental in helping the university recognize the importance of its built heritage. He established the Center for Heritage Conservation within the College of Architecture, a marker program for many of the noteworthy heritage buildings on campus, and guidelines for their care. His knowledge of campus history provides the context for Vosper's designs, and his leadership got this book off the ground.

So, the team was formed, inspired by the images of the buildings, by the spirit of the campus, and specifically by the architectural genius of Vosper, by no means a perfect human being, but who in four short years gave A&M some of its most remarkable buildings.

Our book was a labor of love. It was a labor, like any significant project, but one undertaken with a love for the process of making discoveries together, with a love for the institution the buildings serve, and with the hope that, in sharing what we "see," the Texas A&M University community will find the same delight in the built heritage of the campus and will protect and use it to inspire future generations.

Acknowledgments

ANY BOOK that addresses the history of Texas A&M University owes a debt to Henry C. Dethloff whose 1975 centennial history will always set the bar. The university's Cushing Memorial Library and Archives contains a wealth of textual and photographic materials, and University Archivist Greg Bailey and all his staff, especially Pilar Brackett, who scanned the historical images for this book, were generous with their knowledge, time, and patience. David Chapman, an A&M graduate and former archivist, entertained us literally and figuratively, offering insights into his experiences at the Cushing Library and the development of campus attitudes toward its buildings. Lisa Kalmus, the curator at the Sam Houston Sanders Corps of Cadets Center, graciously provided several historic images. From the College of Architecture, Ian Muise and Phillip Rollfing searched their photographic archives, and Ian and faculty member Marcel Erminy used their photographic skills to record recent architectural work on the campus.

Past and present administrators who offered insights through interviews are recognized in the text and endnotes, but we must also thank Brad Hollas in the Office of Facilities Coordination, Kyle Pole in the Division of Marketing and Communication, and especially University Architect Lilia Gonzales and her team, who never failed to discover facts that had eluded us and provided invaluable guidance for our work.

Recognition that the physical campus was an integral part of the Texas A&M University experience was heightened by the work of the 2004 Campus Master Plan team, Barnes, Gromatsky, Kosarek Architects, with Michael Dennis & Associates. Their in-depth analysis and recommendations set the stage for improvements and procedures that have literally changed the face of the campus. Draft material from the current update by Ayers Saint Gross, overseen by cochairs Dean of Architecture Jorge Vanegas and University Architect Gonzales, contributed to the final chapter of the book. We wish to acknowledge all those who have brought, and continue to bring, their expertise and wise judgment to the Council for the Built Environment and its sub-councils.

For the chapter on Vosper, Michael McCullar's book, *Restoring Texas*, and Katy Capt Whisenant's 1981 thesis on Raiford Stripling provided personal details and quotes from two of the people who knew him best: Stripling and Vosper's son, Bradley, both now deceased. Further helping to bring Vosper out of the shadows was Lila Knight, who was generous with her knowledge and resources, and who transcribed many notes into emails containing information that was not otherwise available to the authors. Cynthia Brandimarte and her staff at the Texas Parks and Wildlife Department—a group whose passion for the Civilian Conservation Corps parks included documentation of Vosper's role as an architect with the National Park Service—made significant contributions. Vosper's drawings and photographs of the state parks are available online thanks to the Texas State Library and Archives Commission. Nancy Sparrow at the Alexander Architectural Archives, who spent many hours looking for Vosper's initials on drawings, and in some cases found them, is deeply appreciated. Her keen eye for his signature and style of rendering people helped uncover the drawings that illuminate Vosper's talent for architectural delineation. Nicole Richard at Columbia University's Avery Library was able to determine that Vosper was not a student at Columbia University, although confirmation of his attending *an atelier* was not forthcoming. The Briscoe Center for American Architecture was also helpful, despite renovations and off-site storage during our research period; our appreciation goes to Vishal Joshi for additional material from that source. Beth Standifird at the San Antonio Conservation Society must be thanked for valuable information on Vosper and Hugo Villa. Work by Stephen Fox on the architecture of Bryan and College Station helped to identify Vosper's contributions to other building projects.

The National Trust for Historic Preservation's Cynthia Woods Mitchell Fund for Historic Interiors, with support from the Center for Heritage Conservation, the College of Architecture, the Department of Biological and Agricultural Engineering, and the College of Agriculture and Life Sciences, provided the grant that supported analysis of the interior finishes of Vosper's work. Special appreciation goes to Matthew Mosca for his willingness to travel far from home to investigate the interiors of these buildings and for the enthusiasm he brought to the project. Kurt and Ted Voss, of Ted Voss Metals, provided photographs and recollections of the company's interaction with Vosper and Villa.

The chapters about specific buildings benefited greatly from the memories and records of building proctors and department heads, often the buildings' greatest champions, and certainly their most vocal representatives on the campus.

The architectural team at Quimby McCoy Preservation Architecture, LLP must be thanked for their research, conducted as part of the firm's work on the Jack K. Williams Building and Scoates Hall Capital Renewal projects, which contributed greatly to the book. Greg Johnston, Andreea Hamilton, and Justin Curtsinger each provided suggestions that led to improvements to the work. Justin Curtsinger, who quickly became the go-to person for knowledge about these two buildings and the history of A&M in general, also prepared the drawings for the book. We are grateful to Marcel Quimby for her willingness to support this effort in the office.

Nancy McCoy wishes to thank Yvonne McCoy for reading the draft, and Mike Hazel, without whom the manuscript would not have been delivered at all; their encouragement is most appreciated. David Woodcock believes that teachers should also be learners, and thanks the several generations of students who contributed to this book by sharing their discoveries about the buildings that surrounded them. The book has provided him an opportunity to express thanks to this remarkable university, and for the understanding and support of his family over all of the years spent on its campus. The authors hope this book will be helpful to new generations of faculty, students, and staff as they make their own journeys around the campus and into its buildings and serve as the stewards of its future.

Finally, thanks to the Texas A&M University Press. We appreciate the enthusiasm of director Shannon Davies; the editorial guidance of senior editor Thom Lemmons and project editor Patricia Clabaugh; the talents of the production and design team, Mary Ann Jacob, Kevin Grossman, and Kristie Lee; and our indexers Peter Brigiatis and Marie S. Nuchols. This book was intended, first, as a celebratory and pictographic look at Vosper's buildings at A&M. Carolyn Brown's photographs of his work were our inspiration.

Architecture That Speaks

1

Building the College

SAMUEL CHARLES Phelps (S. C. P.) Vosper accepted a position at the Agricultural and Mechanical (A&M) College of Texas in the fall of 1929, just over fifty years after the first students enrolled. It is unlikely that he would have set foot on the campus had his professional career not intersected with that of Frederick Ernst (F. E.) Giesecke. And, as a young man, Giesecke would surely not have left his German roots in New Braunfels and come to Brazos County had the A&M College of Texas not existed.

This chapter serves as a broad introduction to the establishment of the college, a task undertaken definitively by historian Henry C. Dethloff in his two-volume, *A Centennial History of Texas A&M University, 1876–1976*.[1] It also describes the life and work of F. E. Giesecke who, as college architect, shaped the physical form of the campus, especially through his interaction with two architects: Samuel Edward Gideon in the opening years of the twentieth century, and later S. C. P. Vosper, the designer of the ten buildings at Texas A&M University that were the inspiration for this book.

Establishing the Agricultural and
Mechanical College of Texas

The genesis of a state college began in 1839, only three years after the Republic of Texas was formed. President Mirabeau B. Lamar noted that, while private education was of great value, the dissemination of knowledge and "the moral and political character of the people . . . must be the work of those higher and more permanent institutions which shall be founded by the nation and directed by public wisdom." Land was set aside by the Fourth Congress of the Republic to support "the establishment and endowment of two Colleges and Universities."[2]

In 1853, seven years after Texas had joined the Union, the newly organized Texas State Agricultural Society called for "an Agricultural College and model farm for the State, at or near the state Capital."[3] In 1858, the State Legislature approved the establishment of The University of Texas, but further action was delayed by the Civil War. The Federal Morrill Land-Grant College Act of 1862 required that, "States accepting the terms of the act must provide, within five years of the date of the act, at least one college where the leading object shall be, without excluding other scientific and classical studies and including military tactics, to teach such branches of learning as are related to agricultural and mechanical arts."[4] Texas accepted this responsibility in November 1866, setting its own five-year deadline for such a college to open its doors in 1871.

Selecting a Site

However, it was not until April 1871 that the state took action to establish The Agricultural and Mechanical College of Texas, appropriated funds for its construction, and decreed that it would be subject to the provisions of the 1858 act that had created the University of Texas, at least in name. The issue of the new college being a branch of the University of Texas, and its access to the endowment income derived from public lands would not be resolved until 1931. However, the process for selecting a site for the new Land Grant College was under way, and received much attention from community leaders in the Brazos Valley.

One of these was Harvey Mitchell, a Tennessee native who moved to Texas in 1839 at the age of eighteen. He taught school for local families, and in 1842 moved to Boonville, the first county seat of Brazos County, to serve as the first deputy in the county clerk's office.[5] The county was a center of cattle and cotton production, and Mitchell and other leaders recognized the value of attracting the new state college to the area. Accordingly, they offered 2,416 acres of land to the commission charged with locating the college, and while there are varying stories as to whether it was a legitimate agreement or the result of a poker game, Brazos County was selected in 1871.[6]

One of the criteria for the siting of the new college was access to a rail line. The Houston and Texas Central Railroad (H&TC) had been organized to link the port of Galveston on the Gulf of Mexico to the agricultural hinterland, and a line was surveyed northward toward the community of Dallas that had been founded in 1839, with a series of townships platted to adjoin the rail line at about twenty-mile intervals. The rail had reached Millican, south of Boonville, when its progress was halted by the Civil War. When work on the H&TC re-commenced, the county seat moved west, to one of the new towns platted by the railway surveyors named after William Joel Bryan, who had donated land for that use. Its prosperity was assured by the arrival of the rail line in 1867, and the town grew rapidly, attracting a wide range of mercantile businesses, hotels, and places of worship, but also gaining a less savory reputation for its many saloons and other forms of worldly temptation.

Ernest Langford, who graduated in architecture in 1913, and served as head of school from 1925 to 1957, and archivist for the college from 1957 to 1971, wrote an unpublished history of the college buildings that was completed in 1963. Langford opens with a story that he admits may be apocryphal, in which the commissioners appointed by Texas Governor E. J. Davis "to select a suitable place for the location of the said Agricultural and Mechanical College," left Bryan and traveled south two and half miles, but remembering how near they were to Bryan with its many distractions for young men, moved south a further two miles or so, and came upon a spot thick with dewberries. Tradition has it that they stuck a stake in the ground and said, "Here we'll build the college."[7] The site was described as, "a wild, bleak prairie, barren of trees and shrubs in its immediate vicinity."[8] The high point of the site marked the watershed between the Brazos and Navasota river basins, a half-mile away from the H&TC line.

Construction Begins

The initial college building program was filled with errors and suggestions of fraud. Architect Caleb Goldsmith Forshey, who had assisted the commissioners in locating the site, was dismissed, and Carl DeGrote was hired to design a building of "elegant and substantial appearance." Many thousands of dollars were expended, but an inspection in late 1871 revealed only an "irregular, not level, cracked and unsafe foundation."[9] The commissioners needed an experienced architect, and turned to Jacob L. Larmour, who had just moved his family and practice to Austin. Larmour was born in New Jersey in 1822, and practiced architecture in New York City until 1857, when he moved to Jackson,

Mississippi. After service in the Confederate cause, Larmour sought other opportunities in Indiana and Minnesota, but recognized that Austin, the newly-named capitol of Texas, would be in need of architectural services, so he moved again. In the 1872–73 City Directory, Austin's first, he is the only architect listed. The end of Reconstruction in 1872 led to much private and public investment, and work was plentiful.[10]

Records that might have described the planning of the original campus were lost in the fire that destroyed Larmour's first building at A&M in 1912. However, the high ridge across the site would have been the natural location for the first building, and the unpaved road that connected it to the HT&C rail line established a major west-to-east axis for the new campus.

On August 6, 1873, Larmour published a request for proposals from contractors and builders for the construction of the building of the A&M College of Texas, at Bryan, Texas.[11] The work was to be bid in separate packages:

1. For the building of a stone foundation.
2. For the making and laying of one million of brick.
3. For all cut stone work.
4. For the carpenter work, the furnishing and laying of floor timbers and making and setting of window frames.

By the end of September, Larmour reported that the first campus building was under way. This main building for the college, quickly named "Old Main," was intended to meet the physical needs of 600 students and their administration, and housed classrooms, offices, library, dining room and kitchen,

Lamour's design of Old Main was typical of the Victorian style favored for public buildings at the time: red brick walls with stone trim and belt courses, double-hung wood windows, a generous decorative wood entrance porch, tiled mansard roof, and twin towers with elegant metal cresting. (Courtesy of Cushing Memorial Library and Archives, Texas A&M University)

and bedrooms, with an assembly room on the fourth floor. The architecture was typical of the Victorian era, four stories tall, with the top floor enclosed in the steep mansard roof. It was constructed of red bricks made on the site. The long hollow running from today's Spence Park to the Association of Former Students Building indicates the source of the clay. The building, perched on the high ridge across the site, looked down to the railroad, and was entered through an imposing two-story wood porch supported by four columns.

In 1875, as the main building was under construction, it was agreed that there was need for living accommodation for a steward, and for proper kitchen and dining facilities. This second building was also to have an attached annex as living quarters for the president of the college and his family. The building, located to the north and west of Old Main, is referred to as "The Mess Hall, three stories high," in the 1882–83 college catalogue. It provided a dining hall some 40 feet by 60 feet on the ground floor, with attendant kitchen and storage facilities. There were student dormitories on two upper floors. Also known as Steward's Hall, it was later named for Thomas S. Gathright, the first president of the A&M College of Texas.

When the A&M College of Texas had its formal opening on October 4, 1876, these were the only two institutional buildings on campus. They were flanked by five "professor's residences," also designed by Larmour, using matching materials and a similar architectural style. The campus, isolated on the prairie, opened with 106 students, referred to as "cadets" (since the Morrill Act required the inclusion of military tactics into the curriculum, and the students wore uniforms of the Confederate south), and a handful of faculty. It was connected to the larger world by the H&TC railroad, whose trains from the north stopped at 12:30 p.m., and those from the south at 4:00 p.m., allowing students and visitors to alight and walk up the incline along a rough drive to arrive at Old Main.[12] It was not until 1883 that the railroad saw fit to construct a depot for the college.

Cadet Frederick Ernst Giesecke Enrolls

The physical form of the campus remained virtually unchanged over the next seven years, so when fourteen-year-old Frederick Ernst Giesecke entered the college in the fall of 1883, this handful of buildings on a barren ridge, 800 yards from the new train

Steward's Hall was completed in June 1876, just four months before the college opened its doors. The attached four-story annex, entered from its own west-facing porch, is referred to in the 1882–83 college catalogue as "the President's residence." After the construction of a separate president's home in 1891, the annex was used to provide housing for college faculty and their families. (Courtesy of Cushing Memorial Library and Archives, Texas A&M University)

depot, Old Main, Gathright Hall, a handful of faculty houses, and some wood-framed workshops would have been the sight that greeted him.

Giesecke was born near Brenham, Texas, on January 28, 1869. His father, Julius Giesecke, had been a captain in Company G, Fourth Texas Cavalry, CSA, and his mother, Wilhelmine Groos Giesecke, was raised in San Antonio. The family moved to New Braunfels in 1873 when Julius was appointed as the technical manager for the New Braunfels Woolen Manufacturing Company. Young Frederick was schooled in New Braunfels from 1876 to 1882, and then entered the German-English School in his mother's hometown graduating in 1883.

Giesecke was, if his autobiography is to be believed, a diligent student at A&M, studying every night and weekend, and was "first in my class, and holding the highest military rank." He notes that when he graduated in 1886, he was awarded medals in physics and in mathematics. The seventeen-year-old was ad-

vised that he might seek a position as a mechanical engineer at the new state capital building in Austin. However, he had noted that one of his instructors needed assistance, so he applied for a position in the college, and was appointed as an instructor in the Mechanical Department at the end of his senior year.[13]

As Giesecke began his teaching career, the college added new buildings to the campus. Eugene T. Heiner of Houston was the second architect to provide professional services to A&M, receiving six commissions between 1887 and 1892. Pfueffer, Austin, and Ross Halls were student dormitories, referred to as "barracks."[14] The first two were simple two-story structures, with Pfueffer located south of Old Main, and Austin placed to the north of Old Main and at an angle to Gathright Hall. Ross Hall was a much grander, three-story Victorian structure, and Heiner located it west of Old Main to the north of the main drive that led from the rail depot. The proximity to Old Main may have encouraged Heiner to follow Larmour's material palette of red

Heiner's Ross Hall, completed in 1891, maintained the architectural style of Old Main and established Abilene Street as the east-west axis of the campus. The photograph from *The Longhorn*, the original name of the A&M yearbook, shows the 1906 football squad. Ross Hall was razed in 1955. (Courtesy of Cushing Memorial Library and Archives, Texas A&M University)

brick, stone trim, and tiled roofs. The three-story barrack building had forty-one rooms on each floor, opening off a central hallway. The central bay had its own hipped roof and finials, and wide wooden porches covered most of the west façade. The interior was sparse, heated only by wood stoves until 1910, the same year that indoor toilets were installed. The rough, unpaved, and as early photographs show, often muddy, road in front of Ross Hall was known as Abilene Street, down which the cadets marched to mess in Gathright Hall.

In 1891, the same year that Ross Hall was constructed, Heiner designed a home for incoming college president Lawrence Sullivan Ross. Early photographs show a typical 1890s Victorian mansion with deep porches and elaborate wooden railings, a highly decorated tower, and steep roofs with gable ornamentation. On a more mundane level, Heiner designed the first shop facilities for instruction in carpentry and iron working.

For his 1889 Assembly Hall, erected to the south of Austin Hall, Heiner introduced a more eclectic style to the campus. Like Ross Hall, the new building was situated on Abilene Street and faced the west. Also referred to as "The Chapel," it was distinguished by twin towers surmounted by Second Empire roofs, with similar shorter towers at its rear. The construction was again brick and wood, but covered on the exterior with cement plaster, scored to resemble masonry. Large arched openings on each façade would have admitted a great deal of light into the interior. Ernest Langford's description of the Assembly Hall was not flattering, referencing the "false quoins, rusticated joints, (and) two meaningless towers on the front," and finding it to be "the most uninteresting structure ever erected on the campus."[15]

Giesecke Becomes the College Architect

In 1888, only two years into his academic career, Giesecke was appointed to head the Drawing Department, and he found himself being asked to design residences for faculty colleagues. Aware that he lacked formal training in architectural design, he spent a summer at Cornell in 1892 studying architectural drawing, heating and ventilating, with a minor in building construction.

While Langford found Heiner's 1889 Assembly Building unattractive, he did find some interest in the three sheet-iron figures superimposed over the pseudo-pediment. "One is engaged in the ancient and honorable vocation of 'turning' a straight furrow, the other two are hammering and sawing away, obviously exercising their talents in the mechanic arts."[16] (Courtesy of Cushing Memorial Library and Archives, Texas A&M University)

On his return, *The Bryan Eagle* reported that "Giesecke was appointed to do architectural work for the college." Beginning with the first power plant in 1893, Giesecke received an official appointment as college architect. This role would find him designing and overseeing the construction of seven buildings between 1893 and 1902, with the majority of the designs being prepared by established Texas architects, including Glover and Allen, Henry F. Jones, and Dodson and Scott.[16] Giesecke did, however, design a residence hall to match Ross Hall in 1899. In keeping with his newfound understanding of architectural symmetry, he located the three-story Foster Hall on Abilene Street to the south of the main drive, forming the first phase of an

"Academic Quadrangle" between the student residences and Old Main.

While mechanical drawing and the application of science to the heating and ventilating of buildings were Giesecke's passions, and his extraordinary capacity for administration and organization allowed him to manage campus construction effectively, Giesecke still had an urge to serve as college architect more directly. He received permission to take a year's leave of absence to study at the Massachusetts Institute of Technology (MIT) in 1903, and returned with a degree in architectural engineering. Armed with his new knowledge, Giesecke created a new architectural engineering curriculum for three of his civil engineering students in 1906, now celebrated as the first architecture program at a state institution in Texas.

Giesecke, ever the engineer, was still fascinated with the heating and ventilating of buildings on a large scale. Seeing the need to expand on his preparation at MIT, he requested a further leave of absence to study at the Technical University of Berlin. This was granted on the basis of half-salary, and he studied in Germany for two terms in 1906 and 1907, developing advanced knowledge of hot water heating systems and of the value of vibrating concrete during the pouring process for the new technique of steel-reinforced concrete construction.[17]

The faculty who taught in the new architectural engineering curriculum staffed the Office of the College Architect, and in the four-year period between 1909 and 1913, they designed and constructed no fewer than seven major buildings.[18] The chief designer for many of these buildings was Samuel Edward Gideon. Six years Giesecke's junior, Gideon was born in Louisville, Kentucky, in 1875, and received his architectural training at MIT between 1904 and 1908, although his obituary notes that he taught at A&M as early as 1900. He studied at Harvard in 1912–13 and attended the *Ecole de Beaux-Arts* at Fontainebleau, France, where he perfected his design abilities. His obituary stated that he taught at A&M between 1904 and 1913, some of the most significant years of the college's early growth. He married Sadie Griffin Cavitt, a daughter of one of Bryan's most prominent families, in 1908.[19]

The first of the buildings in which Gideon played a major role, the Civil Engineering Building, was constructed in 1909. Placed to the southwest corner of Old Main, it established the southern edge of what would become the Academic Quadrangle. Gideon designed the building in a strict Beaux-Arts style. The entrance bay of the front façade projects, with the first floor forming a deep base for four engaged Ionic columns that extend through the second and third floors. It was named for James C. Nagle, the first dean of the School of Engineering, in 1929. In 1912, the Civil Engineering Building was mirrored on the north side of the increasingly significant academic quadrangle by a building for Mechanical and Electrical Engineering. It was subsequently named for a leading professor, and later college president, Frank C. Bolton.

Nagle Hall was the first of a series of buildings designed in the Beaux-Arts tradition that established a new vocabulary for A&M's campus architecture. When Old Main burned during the construction of the Electrical Engineering Building, architect Samuel E. Gideon continued this tradition for the new Academic Building, resulting in a three-building assembly that has anchored the historic core of the campus ever since and, with Ross and Foster Halls, defined the academic quadrangle. (Courtesy of Cushing Memorial Library and Archives, Texas A&M University)

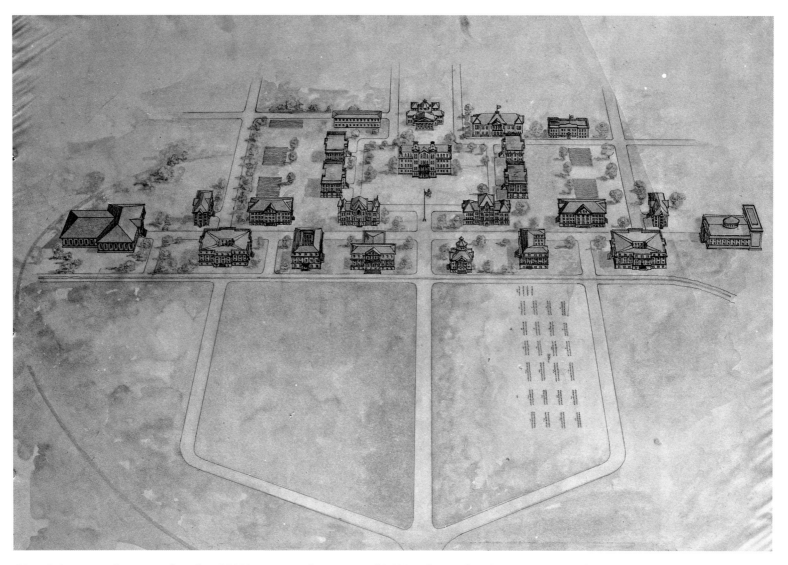

Giesecke's proposed campus plan, dated 1910, envisioned a campus of 2,000 cadets, with a clear west-east axis from the railroad depot to Old Main, and a north-south axis terminating with a mess hall at the north and an assembly building on the south. Ross and Foster Halls appear on his bird's eye perspective, together with most of the buildings extant at the time, with an indication of student formations on the Drill Field. The road pattern from the railroad depot has been maintained into the twenty-first century. The semicircle that defined the Drill Field would be repeated when the campus was reoriented to the east with the design of State Highway 6 in 1930. (Courtesy of Cushing Memorial Library and Archives, Texas A&M University)

The Proposed Campus Plan of 1910

Deciding where to locate these buildings gave the twenty-seven-year-old college architect the opportunity to shape the future physical form of the campus. Giesecke's "Proposed Campus Plan" shows the main access road from the railroad depot, terminating with a flagpole and Old Main, Larmour's 1875 structure. Academic buildings (one the 1909 Civil Engineering Building) flank Old Main, and the late nineteenth-century student residence halls along what was then known as Chapel Street with a mess hall at its north end and an assembly building with a fly tower over the stage at the south end. The date 1910 is shown on a typed legend added to the drawing, but it is interesting that the 1897 Mess Hall, a place of great significance to the cadets and surely a campus landmark, is not shown on the drawing. As it turned out, Giesecke's Campus Plan was both an idealized vision, and prophetically clairvoyant in that disastrous fires in the next two years would allow him to implement key elements of the new plan. The clarity of the concept ensured that its impact would continue through to the twenty-first century.

Implementing the Campus Plan

The 1897 Mess Hall by architects Glover and Allen was northwest of Abilene Street, known as Chapel Street after the 1889 construction of Heiner's Assembly Building since it was used for religious services. Early photographs show cadets in formation marching along the road that angled from Ross Hall. In the early morning hours of November 11, 1911, the Mess Hall caught fire and, being of wood construction except for the brick exterior walls, it was largely destroyed. With a special appropriation from the governor, Giesecke was immediately put to work on the design of a new dining facility to house 2,500 students, which he located as the north terminus of Chapel Street. Giesecke used his new understanding of reinforced concrete construction to create a fireproof building. Gideon's exterior continues the Beaux-Arts tradition, with brick masonry and pilasters, and extensive use of cast stone for three pedimented entrances using Roman Doric columns. The building, at one time claimed

Following the 1911 fire that destroyed the 1897 Mess Hall, the new dining facility, Sbisa Hall, had one main floor and a basement, and defined the north end of Chapel Street, that would be officially named Military Walk in 1915. The photograph, taken about 1920, shows the 1891 president's home and the later Shirley Hotel to the left of Sbisa Hall. (Courtesy of Cushing Memorial Library and Archives, Texas A&M University)

to contain the largest single dining room in the country, was named for Bernard Sbisa who served as supervisor of the Subsistence Division from 1870 to 1926.

In May 1912, construction had hardly begun on the new mess hall, when the college's oldest building, Old Main, also caught fire. Like other buildings of that era, Larmour had used load-bearing brick walls for the exterior shell and some light interior walls, wood framing for each floor and the roof structure, and wood floors, typically maintained with the use of paraffin-based polishes. Old Main burned brightly throughout the night of May 27, with the college records providing additional fuel for the conflagration. The ruined walls were used as target practice by the cadet artillery company, but to little effect, and ropes finally pulled them down.

Thanks to these two disastrous fires, Giesecke's 1910 Campus Plan quickly became a reality, and having established the north terminus of Military Walk with the new Mess Hall, he now had the unique opportunity to remake the central focus of the campus by replacing Old Main, with a grand academic building to house the offices of the president, registrar, commandant, business manager, the exchange store, library, college architect, faculty post office, and various departments of instruction. Giesecke again applied his knowledge of reinforced concrete, though admitted later that he had doubled the quantity of steel bars at the last minute to be on the safe side. The four-story building exhibits the classic Beaux-Arts form with a heavily rusticated base, a two-story central portion with four Ionic columns that rise through both floors, and supporting a pedimented porch whose entablature extends around the building. The visual composition is completed by a fourth floor with a cast stone cornice. All the belt courses, lintels, and cornices use richly ornamented cast stone components with a red-granite aggregate, all of which were made on site. The plan of the building has a wide longitudinal hallway, crossing a central rotunda with twenty-six Doric columns, surmounted by an internal dome and covered by an external copper dome. The brickwork exhibits the same thin bedding joints that Gideon had used on the 1909

Civil Engineering Building. The scale of the building, with its highly articulated cast stone belt courses, pediments, and balcony balustrade, ensured that the new Academic Building, centrally located on the campus and at its highest elevation, would become the iconic structure of the college.

The Academic Building, Giesecke's largest fully reinforced concrete structure, was also Samuel Gideon's crowning design achievement at A&M, before he left to join the faculty at the University of Texas in 1913. Gideon died in Austin in 1945, after a prestigious academic career. During his last months at A&M, he and Giesecke must have worked at lightning speed, for the contract for the Academic Building was approved by the board of directors on August 6, 1912, only nine weeks after the Old Main fire. Giesecke's autobiography simply notes, "At commencement in 1912 we had just finished the plans and specifications for the Academic Building and for Sbisa Hall."[20] At this point, Giesecke had designed or supervised eight major buildings that occupied significant locations on his master plan, and prepared a schematic design for a YMCA Building, the first structure on campus that

The Academic Building was completed in 1914 on the site of Lamour's 1875 Old Main. Gideon's design exemplifies the "base, middle, top" of Beaux-Arts classicism. The majestic scale of the building ensured its significance, and while questions have been raised about the proportions of the copper dome, it remains the signature building of the campus. (Courtesy of Cushing Memorial Library and Archives, Texas A&M University)

was to have a purely social purpose. It was to be located on the north side of the intersection of Main Drive and Abilene Street, another piece of Giesecke's 1910 plan. Simultaneously, he was also developing the design for a sophisticated system to provide central heating for the entire campus. In his centennial history of the university, Henry Dethloff suggests that Giesecke was "overworked and underpaid."[21]

With the Academic Building about to start construction, Giesecke received and accepted an invitation to head the architecture program at the State University in Austin, with the additional offer to continue his own mechanical engineering research and develop a research institute. The board of directors nevertheless appointed him to oversee construction of the Academic Building, taking their cue from Governor Colquitt, who had noted that, "professors (at the university) are not very busy, and Giesecke can do his work (there) and go to College Station from time to time to supervise the work."[22] Giesecke was aided in this oversight role by the appointment of Preston M. Geren as a full-time assistant. Geren had just graduated from A&M, and would later marry Linda, one of Giesecke's daughters. In 1945, their son, Preston M. Geren, Jr., would also graduate in architecture and go on to lead a distinguished practice in Fort Worth.

Therefore, at the end of the summer of 1912, Giesecke left his alma mater, soon to be followed by his chief designer, Sam Gideon, to begin a new phase of his career. The move to Austin would bring Giesecke into contact with Samuel Charles Phelps Vosper, a designer even more remarkable than Gideon, and certainly one more flamboyant and controversial. Within twenty years, that unlikely team would transform the campus of the A&M College of Texas, but for now the college was without its first college architect.

The Campus Without Giesecke

Giesecke's establishment of the Beaux-Arts tradition for design, and his development of the 1910 plan for the campus would continue to guide all future college architects. Student enrollment had hovered between 700 and 900 in Giesecke's last years as college architect, and while the YMCA was much needed

as a social focus for the campus, Giesecke left before his design could be realized. Architect S. J. Fountain refined the design, and the first three floors of the building were completed in 1914. The fourth floor was added in 1920 when additional funds became available. Visitors to the campus traveled along Main Street from the train depot, and climbed a grand stair to a Doric-columned portico that led into a magnificent high-ceilinged room stretching the full width of the building, with an elaborate tiled fireplace on each end wall. Tall windows flooded west light into the space, which was not elaborate, but certainly impressive. The east wing of the building had a half-basement housing the college's first swimming pool, with a two-story chapel approached from the center of the second floor entrance hall, in keeping with the Beaux-Arts tradition of an upper level *piano nobile*.

S. J. Fountain's revision of Giesecke's proposal for the YMCA Building resulted in a meticulously detailed building, completed to the third floor in 1914, with the fourth floor added in 1920. The YMCA remained the center of campus life until the 1950s, and the front steps are recognized as the site of the first pre-football game tradition now known as Yell Practice. (Courtesy of Cushing Memorial Library and Archives, Texas A&M University)

The strong college tradition of selfless service, combined with the requirement for military training, ensured that A&M graduates would play a significant part in serving their country in World War I. The end of that war in 1918 saw the college enrollment jump from 874 in the previous fall to 1,284. As academic programs in agriculture, engineering, and veterinary medicine became more scientific, more students were attracted and enrollment continued to climb rapidly, exceeding 2,000 for the first time by 1923.

Rolland Adelsperger was appointed college architect in 1916, his first project being the College Hospital. He also oversaw the construction of a new assembly building designed by Endress and Watkin of Houston. The building was sited at the south end of Military Walk, completing the vision of Giesecke's 1910 plan. The massive structure was a significant intervention into a neighborhood of single-story faculty homes. The entrance façade facing Military Walk had a tall porch with six finely fluted columns topped by rich Ionic capitols, with similar engaged pilasters on the rear wall of the porch. The bold scale of the design was relieved by the use of terra cotta and hard-pressed brick that allowed for elaborate detailing. The building was completed in 1918, and named for Judge John I. Guion, president of the board of directors. The *Twentieth Biennial Report* of the college describes the 2,500-seat auditorium building as being entirely fireproof and having a dignified Renaissance design.

To meet the needs of a growing student body, the earlier residence halls were joined in 1918 by Adelsperger's Bizzell Hall located west of Military Walk and just north of Guion Hall. The twice-daily practice of cadet formations in front of each residence hall to march to meals in Sbisa Dining Hall at the north and assembly at Guion Hall at the south reinforced the significance of the pedestrian cross-axis in the life of the campus.

As Bizzell Hall was being constructed in 1919, Adelsperger also designed a building to be used for livestock judging. The Animal Husbandry Pavilion consisted of a large open structure with a light, steel-trussed roof spanning 100 feet, and bleacher seating with service accommodation below. Adelsperger decided to use a Romanesque style, with brick facades and grouped ranks of round-headed windows and entrance portals. In 1919, the college was authorized to establish the state's first program in veterinary medicine. Dr. Mark Francis, the legendary founder of the veterinary education program, and for whom the building is now named, laid out the plan for a building to house the program. Adelsperger attempted to expand the use of his Romanesque architecture, but the costs proved prohibitive, and the project was assigned to Endress and Watkin of Houston, who had just successfully completed Guion Hall. Their revisions retained the plan, including the surgical theater on the north side. The final design of the three-story building used simple brick walls, ornamented with Doric and Ionic pilasters on a simple classical façade that faced toward the central axis of the campus. The rear of the building had a long, shallow ramp up which animals could be led to enter a two-story room, apsidal on plan and with bleacher seating, where aspiring veterinarians could observe surgical procedures, illuminated by a large roof light over the operating table.

Adelsperger's term as college architect ended in 1920, after he had added buildings for the Mechanical Engineering and Physics departments. The increasing sophistication of the sciences of agriculture and engineering, and the need to develop practical skills, required additional facilities, even with enrolment staying around 2,500 students. In 1922, college architect E. B. LaRoche added large Mechanical Engineering Shops on the north side of campus, and a four-story Agriculture Building, described by college president W. B. Bizzell in his 1920–21 College Fiscal Report as being "east of, and facing, the Academic Building with its long axis centering on the entrance to the Stock Judging Pavilion." Bizzell noted that, "The exterior walls are of gray brick with stone trimmings, while the style of the architecture harmonized with that of the Academic and other buildings on the campus."

In addition to workshops and classrooms, LaRoche also added buildings that responded to social and physical well-being on the campus, including the Memorial Gymnasium (1924) and

Endress and Watkin's new facility for veterinary medicine used the floor plans devised by Mark Francis, enclosed by a restrained classical façade with simple cast stone details. (Courtesy of Cushing Memorial Library and Archives, Texas A&M University)

the Aggieland Inn (1925). The latter, the only building on campus to favor a Spanish style of architecture, had a brick base, white stucco walls, and red Spanish tile roof. It was described as a modern fireproof hotel with 36 rooms with baths, a large dining room, and a separate cafeteria where meals were served at a very moderate cost. The inn was demolished in 1966 to provide additional parking spaces.

Physical well-being was manifested in organized sports from the earliest days of the college, as can be seen by the college football team lined up in front of Ross Hall (p. v). Agriculture professor Edwin Jackson Kyle assured that his name would be forever associated with A&M football when he allowed the cadets to take over one of his research fields in the southwest corner of the campus early in the twentieth century. Bleachers were erected soon after that time, but by 1927, there was need for a more robust stadium with seating for 35,000 Aggie fans. In 1927, H. N. June, Ernest Langford, and C. E. Sandstedt, architects and engineers, designed a reinforced concrete stadium on a U-shaped plan with long arms open to the south. Arched openings leading to the field were flanked by concrete pilasters

with a simple fluting in Art Deco style. The name, Kyle Field, was cast into the concrete over the central arch.

By the late 1920s, the college consisted of a student body of a 2,500 strong, all-male corps of cadets and a cadre of faculty who lived on campus with their families, with an atmosphere that was partly military college and partly a self-contained village. The community, known to residents in the region as "College," now had a physical facility composed of more than thirty major buildings, including instructional and administration buildings, workshops, a gymnasium and natatorium, shops on campus, and at the Northgate, residences ranging from the brick houses on "Quality Row" for senior faculty and administrators, to smaller wooden houses occupied by other faculty. Faculty members' children growing up on campus enjoyed the run of the place, and had their own school. Servants were housed in even smaller dwellings behind those of the faculty, and the students lived in residence halls.[23] The A&M College of Texas appeared to have arrived at a final state, reflecting F. E. Giesecke's 1910 plan for a campus of 2,000 students.

The aerial photograph, taken soon after the structure was completed, shows the U-shaped stadium open at the south end, with the 1908 natatorium to the north, and the "village" of faculty houses that remained on campus until just before World War II. The 1927–29 reinforced concrete horseshoe remained as the historic core of Kyle Field until it was demolished in 2013–15 to provide for the current stadium that seats 125,000. (Courtesy of Cushing Memorial Library and Archives, Texas A&M University)

Giesecke had suggested a clear plan for the campus in his 1910 bird's eye perspective, and during his absence, his successors followed that organization. The aerial photograph taken in 1925, shows the Hollywood Shacks used for additional cadet housing lined up across from Mitchell Hall and the YMCA, and while the 1922 Agriculture Building is shown on the main axis, the area to its east is sprinkled with a variety of agricultural sheds. What a difference the next ten years would make! (Courtesy of Cushing Memorial Library and Archives, Texas A&M University)

Frederick Ernst Giesecke (1869–1953) is shown toward the end of his life. No other individual has had such an impact on the planning and design of the campus. His 1910 conceptual plan, shown on p. 8, established the organization of the campus that has lasted to the present day, and his support of Samuel Gideon and S. C. P. Vosper established the style and the quality of the buildings in the historic core of the campus. (Courtesy of Cushing Memorial Library and Archives, Texas A&M University)

The Permanent University Fund

As noted in the early part of this chapter, the state legislature had set aside over two million acres of grazing land to provide endowment income for a Permanent University Fund (PUF) for "The University of Texas." However, no institution of that name had been created when the Agricultural and Mechanical College of Texas was established as a "branch" of the unrealized university. Once in place, the University of Texas saw fit to assign only $500 annually from the PUF to support its "branch," a source of considerable discord. In May 1923, when oil was discovered in the Santa Rita field in West Texas, the royalties from the PUF rose to $250,000 per month, and discussions between the University regents and the A&M College directors resumed with greater urgency. It was clear that the "branch college" expected to receive a significantly larger sum in annual support, and that a long-term agreement would have to be reached on the percentage due to each institution. The final discussions were harmonious, since the regents needed the support of the directors to seek a change in the law that would allow revenue from the PUF to be used for the construction of new facilities. While a final legislative agreement was not made until April 8, 1931, both parties were confident of a much greater annual income from the state land endowment, and this affected decisions about new buildings. The 1931 agreement provided A&M with $200,000 a year for three years, beginning September 1, 1934, and one-third of the revenue each year thereafter.[24]

The Winds of Change

In his 1953 autobiography, Giesecke notes, "In 1927 I decided to move from the University (of Texas) to A&M College to become Director of the Engineering Experiment Station so that I could devote my entire time to engineering research; however, circumstances changed this plan and I began my work (back) at the College as Professor of Architecture, College Architect, and Director of the Engineering Experiment Station."[25]

As he had done when he moved from A&M to "the state university" in 1912, Giesecke was able to persuade a gifted architectural designer from the architecture faculty to follow him. In the summer of 1928, with the pace of building about to increase at A&M, Giesecke received word that his former colleague at the University of Texas, Samuel Charles Phelps Vosper, was being released from the faculty in Austin. Eager to add an experienced teacher and accomplished designer to the college, Giesecke offered Vosper a faculty position at A&M, and a role as chief designer in the Office of the College Architect, an offer that Vosper accepted.

Another factor contributed to major changes on the campus at the end of the 1920s. The railroad had continued to bring students and other visitors to the original campus, remaining the prime means of access, and from 1910 to 1923 the college was also served by an interurban rail connection to Bryan, later a bus service, expanding the social and economic opportunities for both communities. Private transportation relied on the horse and buggy, but in 1901, the first automobile appeared in the county.[26] As they increased in number, a state highway network was proposed, including State Highway 6 to link Houston and Dallas, whose path followed the eastern boundary of the campus. On July 4, 1931, the board of directors deeded 7.9 acres of land to be used as the right-of-way, opening up all the land east of the 1922 Agriculture Building for new buildings that could be accessed from the new highway.[27]

So, the stage was set. The campus was reorienting and expanding to the east at a time when several new buildings were proposed. Significant new financial resources were available or could be anticipated from the proceeds of the PUF. Giesecke, with his vision and proven administrative and engineering skills, had returned to A&M. In addition, the Office of the College Architect had gained Vosper, who became known on campus as "Sammy Sunshine," an extraordinary architectural talent. This combination of events would, between 1929 and 1933, provide the A&M College of Texas with ten of its most significant buildings, buildings that have continued to serve and inspire us into the twenty-first century.

2

The Talented S. C. P. Vosper

"SAMMY SUNSHINE" was an architect of tremendous talent, and F. E. Giesecke, whose principal interest at the time was in heating and ventilating systems, needed that talent to carry out what was to be the largest building program to date on the campus. As the principal assistant to the college architect, Vosper contributed his skill as a Beaux-Arts trained architect, his witty personality, and his love of Texas history to ten buildings for the Agricultural and Mechanical (A&M) College of Texas. With the exception of his later work for the National Park Service that the Texas Parks and Wildlife Department has been careful to credit him with and his short-lived practice in partnership with Raiford L. Stripling, very little of Vosper's design work bears his name. Like many designers who do not have an interest in the business or administrative side of architecture, Vosper worked for other architects who were given credit for the projects. However, despite his anonymity in the annals of the historical record, Vosper's buildings are well remembered and often beloved.

The Making of a Beaux-Arts Architect

Samuel Charles Phelps Vosper, also known simply as "Sam" or S. C. P. Vosper, was born May 19, 1887, in New Brunswick, New Jersey, the youngest of five children to John W. and Frances Thompson Vosper, both immigrants to the United States from England and Ireland, respectively. John Vosper worked as the superintendent of a shoe factory and Frances was an amateur watercolorist and painter. As a child, Vosper attended the Trinity Boys School in New York City on a scholarship, which was the foundation for his lifelong engagement in education. At the age of eighteen, he entered Pratt Institute in Brooklyn, New York, to study architecture. After nearly three years, just shy of finishing, Vosper left Pratt due to financial circumstances that were most likely related to the death of his father that same year. Vosper then began working as an architectural draftsman, as did his older brother, James F. R. Vosper, who would remain in the industry as a draftsman, monument designer, and artist.

During this first decade of the twentieth century, a Beaux-Arts education was highly prized, and New York City was the epicenter of Beaux-Arts activity. Architects of means attended the *Ecole des Beaux-Arts* (School of Fine Arts) in Paris, but many American architects learned the lessons of the *Ecole* through participation in an *atelier* that might be available within the larger architectural offices, or an architectural club, led by an experienced, preferably *Ecole*-educated architect, while apprenticing in an office during the day. Vosper participated in more than one *atelier* while he apprenticed with the architectural firm of Electus D. Litchfield Architects for one year and Crow, Lewis, and Wick Architects for nine years. The latter firm specialized in hospital buildings, an expertise that Vosper would put into use later in Texas. According to his professional biography compiled later in life, Vosper also studied at the Beaux-Arts *atelier* of Louis Jallade and for five years with Maurice Prevot.[1] The latter *atelier* was renamed Atelier Corbett in 1912 when Prevot resigned. According to an article in the *Austin American Statesman* in 1923, he eventually became a *Massier*, the leader, of Atelier Corbett, the largest *atelier* in New York City. In the article, Vosper credits himself with mentoring two successive Paris Prize winners in this leadership role. Harvey Wiley Corbett (1873–1954) was an *Ecole*-trained architect associated with Columbia University, first as the head of an *atelier* and later as a teacher. The Columbia University Extension Atelier had several studios in New York at this time. At least one of Vosper's *projets* (proposed design), titled "Entrance to an Office Building," was exhibited at the twenty-ninth annual exhibition of the Architectural League of New York and published in the accompanying catalog in 1914.[2]

In addition to his *atelier* work, Vosper studied oil painting with August Schwabe; life drawing at the Arts Student League; theater design under Theodore Van Crua, designer of the Metropolitan Opera House in New York; and architectural rendering with Birch Burdette Long. Long (1878–1927), who is said to have influenced the rendering style of Frank Lloyd Wright, was one of the best-known architectural graphic artists in the United States.[3] It is not known for how long and under what circumstances he studied with Long, who was also an authority of color theory, but architectural rendering and color were two of Vosper's strengths. This combination of training in drawing and painting, color theory, the Beaux-Arts atelier activities, and an apprentice position produced a very well-rounded young architect of his day.

Vosper met Augusta L. Westerfield, member of an old New York family, through singing in a church choir, and the two were married in 1914.[4] Their first son, David, reportedly died as an infant after falling from his high chair. In 1917 the couple's second son was born, whom they also named David. The family, which included a seventy-five-year-old grandmother named Lucy McMahon, lived with a boarder named Percy and a married couple from England on Staten Island in a house that still stands at the end of a cul-de-sac. However, domestic stability would not last long.

Vosper had a proclivity for travel, perhaps in search of good work, adventure, and a good time, and this lifestyle was difficult to sustain with a family. The first trip away from home occurred just a year after his second son's birth, when an opportunity to design a lavish real estate development for the Packard family led Vosper to move to Jacksonville, Florida, with the expectation that his wife and son would soon join him. Sadly, the opportunity was not realized and Vosper ended up designing only a Tea House.[5] Vosper's 1917–1918 Draft Registration Card indicates that he was working for L. P. Hutton, in Orlando, Florida, as an architect and that he supported his wife, child, and grandmother; his physical description is "tall, slender, blue eyes, dark brown hair," and his family's address is still in Staten Island. However, Vosper stayed in Florida, where he also worked for architect R. A. Benjamin on theaters, and eventually found himself specializing in designing theaters for A. Lynch Enterprises and the related Southern Enterprises, and Famous Players-Lasky Corporation, which required traveling across the country. Among the many theaters he designed are Palace Theatres in Jacksonville, Florida, Charlotte, North Carolina, and Little Rock, Arkansas.[6] It was this work that eventually led him to Dallas.

A. Lynch Enterprises, Southern Enterprises, and Famous Players-Lasky Corporation were rapidly acquiring theaters in 1918–19, around the time Vosper began to work with them. The latter company would soon become the "largest concern in the motion picture industry and the biggest theater owner in the world," according to the Federal Trade Commission when it accused the company of restraint of trade in violation of antitrust laws in 1921.[7] Possibly as a result of the turmoil surrounding the antitrust suit, Vosper, who was brought to Dallas by Famous Players-Lasky, ended up working for Herbert M. Greene Company instead, a position that would serve him very well over the next three decades that he would spend primarily in Texas. His family remained in New York, however, until the birth of his third son, Bradley Moffet, in 1921, after which Augusta and the two boys moved to Texas.

The Making of a Texan

Vosper lived in the Oak Cliff area of Dallas when he began working for Herbert M. Greene Company. Within the year, he was a founding member of the Dallas Architectural Club, a Beaux-Arts *atelier* that was established in 1920, and served as its *Massier*, where he mentored and taught younger architects the traditions of Beaux-Arts design. In 1922, Vosper won the club's "Silver Award," its highest honor. While in Dallas, he met David Williams, a well-known architect who became a lifelong friend and with whom Vosper shared an interest in historic preservation, or restoration as it was more commonly called at that time.[8] Williams and Vosper were also both accomplished artists whose paths surely crossed at the Dallas Architectural Club.

One of Vosper's projects while working for Greene was the Eastern Star Home (1924, demolished) in Arlington, for which Ralph H. Cameron was the associate architect. The Eastern Star Home was a Georgian-style boarding house, very similar in appearance to Greene's Lincoln House in Dallas, completed in 1921. Cameron and Greene collaborated on many projects, including the Scottish Rite Cathedral in San Antonio. One or both of these projects must have led to Vosper's move to Cameron's office in San Antonio in 1923, where his family joined him.

Not long after moving to San Antonio, Vosper began teaching at the University of Texas (UT), commuting to Austin to do so. He was first listed as a lecturer among the faculty in 1923, iron-ically a year during which Giesecke, who was then chairman of the Architecture Department within the College of Engineering, was on leave. Giesecke must have had an opportunity to know Vosper, however, because he prepared a handwritten resolution to the university's board of trustees in support of Vosper's reinstatement that year that included this recognition: "Vosper has raised the standard of work in the department to an extent demonstrated by the fact that of the projects submitted by UT to the Beaux-Arts Institute of Design in New York City this year and heard from to date, seventy-eight percent received awards as compared to twenty-five percent which received awards last year."[9] The resolution was signed by a long list of students. Vosper served as a lecturer for 1924 through 1926, and in 1927, he was identified as an associate professor for the first time. That same year, the *Austin American Statesman* reported, quoting Vosper, that the university had received the best recognition ever given to a student from the Society of Beaux-Arts Architects.

Robert Leon White, who worked briefly with Vosper in Cameron's office, was hired by the university at the same time as Vosper, but as an adjunct professor and a year later as associate professor and superintendent of construction for the university's building program that Herbert M. Greene Company was designing. The intersecting careers of Vosper and these three men—Greene, Cameron, and White—put him in the company of several of the most successful architects in Texas at the time.

While commuting to Austin to teach, Vosper was living with his family in San Antonio and busy in Cameron's office. Both the Eastern Star Home and the Scottish Rite Cathedral were completed in 1924. Vosper's daughter, Janice Gracel, was born in San Antonio in 1925 while the family lived in a Craftsman-style bungalow located at 302 Hermitage Court.

The Cathedral opened to great fanfare and Vosper was proud of his work on this building, where his theater experience had been an asset. As reported by the *San Antonio Express*:

> The designers of the building have literally ransacked the resources of modern architecture to make the building an enduring monument and an outstanding ornament to the City of San Antonio. S.C.P. Vosper, who, under Mr. Greene,

Greene, Cameron, and White

Herbert M. Greene

Herbert M. Greene (1871–1932) established his architectural practice in 1897 upon moving to Dallas from his native Pennsylvania, where he graduated with a bachelor of science in architecture from the University of Pennsylvania in 1893. In 1900, he entered into a partnership with James P. Hubbell to form Hubbell and Greene. In 1918, he formed Herbert M. Greene Company, the firm that Vosper joined in 1920. In 1922, Greene became the principal university architect for UT, where he designed eight significant buildings prior to his position being taken over by Paul Phillipe Cret in 1930. Greene maintained a collaborative relationship with Cameron, who served as associate architect for some of Greene's projects. Some of the UT buildings constructed under Greene's leadership include the Texas Memorial Stadium (1924), Biology Building (1925), Recitation Building (Garrison Hall, 1926), Wooldridge Hall (1924; demolished 2010), Littlefield Memorial Dormitory (Littlefield Residence Hall, 1927), Gregory Gymnasium (1930), and Chemistry Building (Welch Hall, 1931). In 1923, Greene formed Greene and LaRoche with partner Edwin Bruce LaRoche, and in 1926, George Dahl joined them, becoming a partner in 1928 to form the firm of Greene, LaRoche, and Dahl.

Ralph Haywood Cameron

Ralph Haywood Cameron (1892–1970) was born and practiced in San Antonio his entire career, starting at age 13 in the office of Alfred Giles and at 14 with Adams and Adams. He opened his own practice in 1914. The firm's best known buildings include the Medical Arts Building (1926) and the US Post Office and Courthouse (1937) next door, for which he served as associate architect with Paul Cret. While recuperating from an injury when serving in the US Army during World War I, he studied briefly at the *Ecole des Beaux-Arts* at Fontainbleau. Cameron was instrumental in establishing the Texas Society of Architects and served as its first president. He became a Fellow of the American Institute of Architects in 1937. Cameron collaborated often with Herbert M. Greene, and some of those projects are ones that Vosper has been identified with and likely the reason for the connection between Vosper and Cameron. Projects include the Eastern Star Home in Arlington and the Scottish Rite Cathedral in San Antonio. Vosper became a partner with Cameron and was the principal designer on some of the firm's best-known buildings during the period between 1923 and 1929. Vosper rejoined Cameron's by 1951.

Robert Leon White

Robert Leon White (1898–1964) was born near Cooper, Texas, and graduated from UT in 1921. He worked for Cameron and for Phelps and Dewees as a draftsman before moving back to Austin to teach in 1923. White became the superintendent of construction at UT a year later and was appointed supervising architect in 1926, a position he held until 1958. During the period 1923–30, White worked closely with Greene. He also designed several buildings for the university, including the Student Union building. After 1930, White worked closely with Cret and associated architect Ralph Cameron on the impressive building program of the 1930s. White collaborated with Cameron and Vosper on the Central Christian Church of Austin (1928). He was also responsible for and collaborated with Vosper on the outpatient building at the John Sealy Hospital (1931–32), the Rebecca Sealy Nurses Residence (1933), and the Crippled Children's Hospital (1937) in Galveston. White took a leave of absence from his position at UT to join Vosper and Stripling in Goliad from 1934 to 1937 to work on the Mission Nuestra Señora del Espíritu Santo de Zuñiga, after having written a thesis for his master's degree in 1930 on the San José y San Miguel de Aguayo Mission in San Antonio.

drew the plans for the interior of the building, and who has had a wide experience in designing some of the leading theaters of the country, says that the stage and electrical equipment will equal many of the big metropolitan theaters of the United States.[10]

During this time, Vosper considered the Cathedral his most noteworthy building. He designed it and did all the mechanical layouts, including an elaborate lighting system and innovative acoustical treatments. He also incorporated a novel movable floor feature that was considered so good that it was adopted, just before construction was completed, by the largest of the Scottish Rite Cathedrals located in Detroit. He was now in partnership with Cameron and reportedly had $3 million worth of work in progress, including the two projects with Greene's office, the Medical Arts Building, and a Municipal Auditorium.[11] Like many of Vosper's designs, the Scottish Rite Cathedral was recognized with listing on the National Register of Historic Places in 1996.

However, the building that would get the most attention then and now is the Medical Arts Building, completed in 1926, just a block from the Cathedral and across the street from Alamo Plaza. This building takes cues from New York's famous Flatiron Building (1902), with its similar wedge shape. The narrow end faces the Alamo and the Gothic-style decoration, complete with apparently ill gargoyles, that are almost the antithesis of what would be expected of a medical office building. This building quickly became a landmark. It was converted to the Landmark Office Building in 1978 and to the Emily Morgan Hotel in 1985. Not surprisingly, it is rumored to be the second most

This rendering is believed to be an early study for the Medical Arts Building and serves as a good example of Vosper's drawing technique in pencil. While many of Vosper's renderings are not signed, this one has the initials in the bottom middle of the image. (Courtesy of the Alexander Architectural Archives, The University of Texas Libraries, The University of Texas)

The Medical Arts Building as it appeared in 2015. Decoration is unrestrained, with gargoyles and other Gothic-style ornament mixed with storks and medical references.

These two "patients" face one another in misery, to everyone's delight.

photographed building in San Antonio. The building became a formal landmark with its listing on the National Register of Historic Places as a part of the Alamo Plaza Historic District in 1977 and as a City of San Antonio local landmark.

For the design of the Central Christian Church in Austin, completed in 1929, Vosper and Cameron collaborated with White, a member of the congregation. While Vosper's name does not appear on the architectural drawings, which means he is technically not credited with the design, he did get his name onto the cornerstone of the building with the other two men. However, Vosper's hand is evident in the design of this building. This Romanesque Revival–style church employs nearly all of the materials that would be used in the buildings Vosper designed for the A&M College of Texas, and his wit, so often found in the details of his buildings at A&M, is here too. The Central Christian Church was designated a Registered Texas Historic

On this pencil rendering of the Central Christian Church in Austin, Vosper's mark takes on the more unusual form at the bottom right of the image. Vosper has taken all four of his initials and superimposed them to create what appears to be a flower but is, in fact, his signature. This particular signature is also found on a rendering of the Women's Gymnasium at The University of Texas at Austin. (Courtesy of the Alexander Architectural Archives, The University of Texas Libraries, The University of Texas)

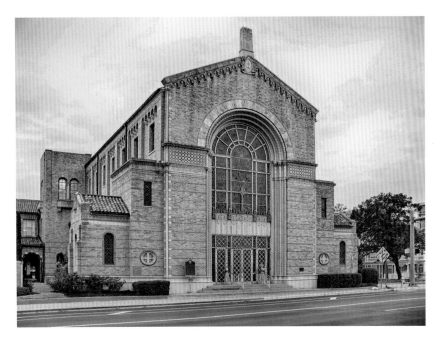

The church as it appeared in 2015 (*above*). Within the style-appropriate treatment of the very ornate ironwork entrance, Vosper has included a series of little flower pots in place of more traditional elements (*right*). (Photographs by Nancy T. McCoy)

Landmark in 1985 and was listed on the National Register of Historic Places in 1992.

While his architecture may be beautiful, other parts of Vosper's life were not. In *Restoring Texas, Raiford Stripling's Life and Architecture*, Michael McCullar recounts a less-than-flattering portrait of him, but with unquestionable respect for his talent from nearly everyone who recorded an opinion. McCullar's book contains stories told by an architect from San Antonio named Bartlett Cocke who worked as a young draftsman with Vosper in Cameron's office in 1926. Cocke recalls Vosper as a "very peculiar individual. There were six people working for Cameron then, and Cameron kept Vosper in one corner of the room, away from everyone else." Cocke reports that Vosper looked older than he was, his teeth were bad, and he seemed to "abuse himself" smoking and drinking too much and working late at night. Cocke continues: "And his level of production was

somewhat irregular, depending not so much on the volume of work in the office as his own level of inspiration. But when he worked he was brilliant. He could turn out the most magnificent designs and renderings—and without the kind of brooding, sensitive ego that creative people often have. He laughed a lot—at himself as well as others—and everyone liked him."[12]

One day Cocke decided to ask Vosper what the initials "S. C. P" stood for. "He looked at me in that jolly way of his and said 'Somewhat Chemically Pure,' and then he'd laugh and snort and carry on." Vosper was also self-deprecating and uninterested in personal acclaim. Cocke recalls when Vosper was designing the Medical Arts Building and drew a beautiful rendering of the project, then signed it "M. O. Frank," the name of a young woman just out of school working in the office as a draftsman.[13]

Meanwhile, in 1927, Frederick Ernst Giesecke left UT to return to A&M to serve as director of the Texas Engineering

Experiment Station, head the building program as college architect, and to lead the Department of Architecture. The timing of this new position allowed Giesecke to avoid at least two scandals involving the architecture department faculty at UT. The first incident occurred in April 1928 when a professor was accused of "the making of intoxicants and the partaking in said intoxicants with students" and quickly relieved of his position. Professors Gideon and Vosper were brought in to take over the teaching duties, a solution that is not entirely without irony in Vosper's case.[14] In May of the same year, Vosper himself was the subject of controversy when he was fired for using a nude model in a life drawing class that involved the Visvakarma Club, a group that included faculty, students, and other persons with an interest in a variety of artistic endeavors. In an effort to save Vosper's position, Robert Leon White wrote a two-page letter to President H. Y. Benedict outlining the importance of Vosper to the Department of Architecture and encouraging him to suspend rather than terminate Vosper:

> It is a matter of record that the Department of Architecture owes its present high standing and ranking, as a member of the American Collegiate Schools of Architecture and rank as one of the leading schools of Architecture in America, to Mr. Vosper's ability and work in teaching design. The Department had repeatedly applied for recognition to this body and each time been turned down with the criticism that the school was weak in design. Within two years from the time Mr. Vosper took over the senior design work he had raised the standard of the work turned out to such an extent that the department was immediately recognized and granted admission. . . . As for example, the past year his students won eight medals in the Beaux-Arts Institute of Design Competitions, not to mention a great number of First Mentions in all competitions. These represent the highest awards given students in this work and a record any Professor in Architectural Design might well envy. Before he took over this work no such awards were ever won, in fact the advanced problems were not even attempted by the instructors and students here. . . . He has in his

zealousness and interest in instilling Architecture in the students, erred. This was a great mistake and one to be regretted. He was reared in the art schools in New York and consequently did not realize the difference, perhaps.[15]

Vosper disappears from the minutes of faculty meetings after May 2, 1928.

Prior to his leaving the university, Vosper's credentials and Beaux-Arts-style teaching skills made a strong impression on Giesecke, who had hired him in the first place. Giesecke was so impressed that after the first year, for much of which Giesecke was on leave of absence, he was willing to write the resolution in support of Vosper's reinstatement for a second term. Giesecke was the second chairman of the Architecture Department at UT for a period from 1912–27. Under his leadership, the department finally gained membership in the Association of Collegiate Schools of Architecture. Vosper and White, who were both added to the faculty in 1923 to boost the program after it had failed to attain that membership the previous year, were a significant part of the department's success and White gave most of the credit to the more senior Vosper. So, it is not surprising that when Giesecke decided to return to A&M in late 1927, he thought to bring along Vosper to help him to teach and to serve as his chief designer. It would take Vosper two more years to arrive in College Station however.

The *Bryan Daily Eagle* reported on the appointments of both Giesecke and Vosper to the A&M College in September 1927, suggesting they arrived at the same time.[16] Yet records of the minutes of faculty meetings in 1927–28 at UT have Vosper in attendance through May 2, 1928. Furthermore, the *Austin American Statesman* put Vosper in Austin and San Antonio during this period with reference to his position at UT. An article on July 20 refers to Vosper "whose connection with the university architecture department is being disputed," and by November 8, he is referred to as a "former professor."[17] However, assuming he was available to take on the position at A&M as early as November 1928, he was not officially appointed by the A&M board of directors as a professor until September 29, 1929, a full two years after his position was announced.

It is unclear exactly when Vosper made it to College Station, but there were some extenuating circumstances that might have interfered with his arrival. Tragedy struck on August 23, 1928, when Vosper's eleven-year-old son David died of accidental blood poisoning from a superficial cut. Younger son Bradley recalled that his father would never be the same.

> Although he retained his cheerfully outgoing demeanor, he would never again be as happy-go-lucky as he was before David's death. And although he had always been rather "proper" in a bohemian sort of way, taking pleasure in the finer things in life—good eating, clothing, art, and music—Vosper fought depression with too much food and drink and grew even more careless about his appearance, his over-six-foot frame gaining more weight than it was designed to carry.[18]

When Vosper left San Antonio for College Station, he left the remainder of his family behind once again. His wife, Augusta, moved to Austin, where she resided at several different addresses between 1929 and 1935. In the 1930 US Census, Augusta is listed as being 39 years old and as the "head of household," living with son, Bradley, then eight, and daughter, Janice, then four. Augusta had no occupation and was living at 1118 West 7th Street as a renter. Hence, during a marriage that began in 1914, Vosper lived away from his family from 1917 to 1923 and then left again by 1929. This would be the end of the marriage, although son Bradley told McCullar that the couple never officially divorced.

The Four Years in College Station

As a teacher, Professor Vosper was by all available accounts very well-liked by his students. He brought with him the Beaux-Arts approach to teaching architecture, staying up late with his students and sending their drawings to the Beaux-Arts Institute of Design in New York for judging, a practice that students appreciated. Professor S. J. Fountain, who had studied at the *Ecole des Beaux-Arts* and became department head in 1912, when Giesecke left for UT, had introduced Beaux-Arts training to

A&M. Fountain died in 1914, and it was not until the late 1920s that the college took up Beaux-Arts training again. According to Ernest Langford, the head of the Architecture Department from 1929 until 1956, enthusiasm for this style of training had waned but "began to bud again in the middle and late twenties," reaching "full bloom once more under the direction of S. C. P. Vosper, one of the ablest delineators of modern times. . . . Few men could equal him in the composition of a '*projet;*' none surpassed him in his brilliant use of colors in presentations."[19]

In 1929, Ernest Langford (1887–1963) joined the faculty of A&M and succeeded Giesecke as department head, while Giesecke remained in the role of college architect and head of the Experiment Station. Langford '12 served 27 years as head of the architecture department and 23 years as mayor of College Station. Although he recognized Vosper's talent for rendering and teaching, Langford was not his fan, personally or professionally, referring to his loose morals, slovenly appearance, and bad habits. Langford did not particularly care for Vosper's architecture either, finding it too gaudy, colorful, and overdesigned. The single exception was the Administration Building, which Langford applauded.

Despite some poor habits, Vosper was prolific, producing designs for ten remarkable buildings that were designed and built in only four years. When he arrived on the A&M campus, the first phase of the Chemistry Building and Cushing Library were already designed, but construction had not yet begun on the library. Dormitories were a high priority due to a serious housing shortage on campus and funding for Hart Hall was appropriated on the same day Vosper was officially appointed. Walton Hall would follow, using funds the college created through an increase in rent. The remaining seven buildings, including the second phase of the Chemistry Building, were funded with approximately $3 million in oil money after protracted discussions with UT as to A&M's share of monies from the Permanent University Fund. Vosper's role on the Cushing Library design was primarily felt on the interior of the building and is recounted by the head cataloguer for the Library who provided many details about the design and construction process. The remainder of the buildings bear Vosper's distinct fingerprint. All of them "speak" about their purpose and feature cast stone ornament of superior quality, vividly colorful Mexican tile, and interiors that include elaborately decorated spaces rivaling the best commercial interiors anywhere in the United States. These buildings also continue the tradition of Beaux-Arts style that had been introduced to the campus two decades earlier by Giesecke. The unique circumstances of the influx of funding, low cost of labor during the Depression and hence, the availability of building craftsmen, and Vosper's own talent made this exceptional collection of buildings possible.

The office of the college architect consisted of 31 employees in 1931, including architects, landscape architects, and structural and mechanical engineers. They were housed in Ross Hall, a former dormitory and one of the oldest buildings on campus. Curiously, in November 1929, Giesecke had pronounced Ross Hall as unfit for students to live in and called for it to be razed, but apparently the need to find space for a growing cadre of professionals in the college architect's office kept it functioning a while longer. Giesecke's office was on the first floor, engineers were located on the second floor, and Vosper and the other architects

This 1925 photograph depicts the campus as it would have generally appeared when Vosper arrived, before the start of the building program. Ross Hall is the pitch-roofed structure to the immediate left of the sidewalk leading to the Academic Building entrance. Directly across the street from Ross Hall is the YMCA building. The back of the YMCA building and the front of Ross Hall face Military Walk, which runs north-south.
(Courtesy of Sam Houston Sanders Corps of Cadets Center, Texas A&M University)

worked on the third floor. Vosper's residence was across Military Walk on the third floor of the YMCA building, where there were rooms for rent. Classes on architecture were held nearby on the fourth floor in the Academic Building.

A couple of years after Vosper's arrival, Giesecke, who by then must have been aware of Vosper's afflictions, hired one of Vosper's former students to help ensure that he showed up for work each day. The former student was Raiford L. Stripling '31, who had gone to Tyler to work upon graduation but returned for this unusual job description six months later. Stripling and Vosper had established a close student-mentor relationship and a friendship that made Stripling's new position possible. The job required special skills, described by Giesecke as follows:

> Now you be Mr. Vosper's personal assistant, and the biggest job you have is to go up ever [sic] mornin' and get him up and get him to work as soon as you can. . . . Now, I don't want you to try to get him there at any certain time. Just *get* him there everyday.[20]

For Stripling, the job was a little different:

> Now sometimes in the mornin' I'd have to give him about two shots of booze to get him out of bed, but if that was required, I'd do it.[21]

Another part of his job was to draw the full-size details that were used to create the cast stone ornament on the buildings, and eventually Vosper came to trust him enough to allow him to design one of the entrances to the Administration Building, among other things. The men often worked long hours, at fifty cents an hour in Stripling's case, and often late at night. In addition to Stripling were architects and landscape architects Leo (probably Phillip) Norton, "Happy" Padgett, John Astin Perkins, and Elo Urbanovsky. Vosper came to be known as a special campus character as well as a brilliant designer. He was given the nickname "Sammy Sunshine," despite the fact that he apparently preferred to work during the night. These young men and Vosper not only worked together by day and sometimes by night, but they also paid regular visits to the bootlegger to replenish their stock of Prohibition booze and visited nearby Calvert, Texas, for late-night dancing. In Stripling's words, "Yeh, Vosper hit the booze real good. That's something else he and I agreed on. He'd always have something to drink, and I could keep up with him. Then I'd drink him under the table, 'cause he'd get drunk and I wouldn't."[22]

Construction for the building program was handled using the college's own forces, known as the Department of Building and College Utilities. Students as well as college employees provided the labor. Construction superintendent William A. Orth was responsible for construction projects. In November 1931, Orth requested and was granted approval to make cast stone on campus. Employees provided trades such as carpentry and painting while specialty trades like ornamental iron or steel were bid to contractors. Likewise, the Office of the College Architect, Giesecke, and his staff of engineers and architects handled the design of the buildings. The first phase of Chemistry, Cushing Library, Hart, and Walton Halls were all built under this system. As the board of directors began to appreciate the potential funding that was to benefit A&M once its share of the oil money was ironed out with UT, they recognized the enormity of this building program and took another step to ensure its success. In July 1931, the board directed Giesecke to submit all preliminary plans to W. J. Smith of Childs and Smith Architect in Chicago, who was retained as consulting architect.

However, as the agreement with UT was finalized, this process for building came under criticism from both the architectural and construction industries. The board of directors listened to industry leaders at a special meeting in Houston on January 24, 1932. Architecture and construction representatives stated why they thought hiring private architects and engineers and bidding to contractors was a better policy. Ralph Cameron of San Antonio was one of those who noted the importance of giving students practical exposure to the design and construction process, that it was taxpayers' money and that the college taught good architecture and design but did not practice it. Some of

Raiford Leak Stripling

Raiford L. Stripling (1910–90) of St. Augustine, Texas, graduated with a degree in architectural design from A&M College in 1931 and found a job in Tyler, Texas, the only student in his class to do so as jobs were hard to come by at the beginning of the Depression. Stripling won an American Institute of Architects award for academic achievement his junior year and a gold medal in the last annual F. O. Witchell drawing competition his senior year, a competition of A&M students sponsored by the Dallas-based firm Lang & Witchell. Vosper came to teach at A&M in the last years of Stripling's studies and, realizing the special mentor-student relationship that had developed between the two men, Giesecke hired Stripling to help Vosper with the building program. A lifelong friendship ensued that included a business partnership that lasted into the 1940s. The men worked together on the restoration of the Mission Nuestra Señora del Espíritu Santo de Zuñiga at Goliad State Park and other projects. The Mission project introduced Stripling to historic preservation, a specialty field within architecture that Stripling practiced his entire career. Some of his prominent restoration projects include the Ashton Villa in Galveston, Independence Hall at Washington-on-the-Brazos, and the Presidio Nuestra Senora de Loreto de la Bahia in Goliad. Michael McCullar's *Restoring Texas* provides an in-depth account of Stripling's life and career, with many references to Vosper.

the speakers went so far as to state that students of the college might not get jobs when they graduated due to their exposure to poor construction projects. Other comments included the concept that the college was losing friends in pursuing the current policy.

The board voted to maintain the college architect and his staff in the design role but to begin bidding the construction projects, with the provision that Orth be given the same opportunity to bid as anyone else. This practice started with the Petroleum Engineering and Geology Building. Following that, the Agricultural Engineering Building was bid but had to be partially redesigned to eliminate two window bays at the rear wing and a crane that was designed into the building in order to lower the costs. The preferred bidder for the Animal Industries and Veterinary Hospital begged the board not to hire him for both projects because he had under-bid the jobs; his bids were returned to him. Despite these difficulties, the board continued

bidding the construction and the hiring of students for construction purposes.

The Depression was in full effect during this time. Employees of the college took pay cuts of 10 and 20 percent in 1933. While the Depression was felt on campus, jobs were available and the building program contributed significantly to the local economy. On March 4, 1933, Franklin Roosevelt was inaugurated, and less than a month later, the Volstead Act was repealed, enabling the sale of beer and wine as determined by voting in state precincts. Beer was approved for most of Brazos County, but hard liquor—Vosper's preference—required driving west into adjacent Burleson County. Bryan had a few watering holes, but liquor was not allowed on campus. Apparently, some campus residents managed to have it on campus nonetheless.[23] In October 1933, as the Animal Industries Building, the last of the ten buildings, was being completed, Vosper and Stripling left town and headed for San Antonio.

The Preservation Architect

Vosper found an opportunity for himself and Stripling to work for the Civil Works Administration (CWA) in San Antonio, where the two men lived in an old Spanish home and worked on the design of city park facilities—bathhouses and shelters. After about seven months in San Antonio, both men were transferred to the CWA office in Austin, where they met up with architect David Williams, Vosper's friend from Dallas who shared his interests in architectural rendering, regional architecture, and historic preservation

Next, Vosper took a job with the National Park Service (NPS), which was spearheading a new movement to save historic buildings across the United States, soon to become national policy with the passage of the Historic Sites Act of 1935. During this time, the agency was employing architects to design parks in some of the most beautiful natural settings that had been set aside by the states for preservation. Money for these programs became available to Texas in 1933 and formed a group of parks that became the basis for the Texas Park and Wildlife Department's (TPWD) network of state parks.[24] The Civilian Conservation Corps (CCC) facilitated the building of these parks, using a workforce of young men who were housed in camps all over the state and built park facilities based on NPS architects' designs and using local materials. This highly successful program produced some of the most magnificent parks and park architecture in Texas.

Vosper had the opportunity to work on two of these parks: first at the Longhorn Caverns State Park No. SP-35 in Burnett and later at Goliad State Park No. SP-43 in Goliad. Documentation of Vosper's role on both of these sites is excellent, as the TPWD maintains records and has a keen interest in preserving the CCC contributions to the state's park system. At Longhorn Caverns, Vosper designed the main administration building that sits above a dramatic staircase entrance to the caverns. The custodian's dwelling in this park is also thought to be Vosper's design. The original architectural drawings for the administration and other built improvements at this and other state parks under

this program are available through the Texas State Libraries and Archives Commission online and through programs related to interpretation of the CCC-built state park through the TPWD. This park was listed on the National Register of Historic Places as part of the Park Road 4 Historic District in 2011.

This design at the Longhorn Caverns State Park demonstrates how architects like Vosper were trained to design in any style; in this case it is National Park Service Rustic. The general character of park structures was prescribed by the federal agency, which also assigned personnel to ensure the standards were met. (Photography by Nancy T. McCoy)

This photograph of Big Bend was taken by Vosper in 1934, around the same time as his commission to make watercolor paintings, and was annotated with the notes "Clouds of Big Bend" and "Alpine, Texas." The image is part of a large collection of Vosper's photographs, many of which are unlabeled, that were taken between circa 1926 and circa 1936 of the landscape and rural buildings in southern and south-central Texas and in Mexico. Many of these images came from trips taken by Vosper and Stripling to places such as the Mexican border towns of Camargo and Mier. Photography was also an artistic venture; as reported by McCulllar, Stripling recalled that Vosper once spent half a day photographing nothing but cloud formations and the sky. (Courtesy of Cushing Memorial Library and Archives, Texas A&M University)

As reported by Stripling to Katy Capt in 1981, Vosper was working for the NPS and had been assigned the task of creating watercolor paintings of Big Bend, which was being nominated as a national park at the time. Without enough money to get there, Vosper dropped in on the office of Robert Leon White, with whom Vosper had arranged a job for Stripling, to get some help from his former students. As told by Stripling:

When Vosper was commissioned to go to the Big Bend to make a series of watercolors . . . he had an old Model A Ford coupe that he had to drive out there. He came up to White's office and more than half of the personnel [there] had been students of his either at UT or at Texas A&M. And he said, "Boys, I have to have some money. I have to go to the Big Bend." So we put in all the money we could raise among about eight of us and . . . one of his UT students and I went to the bookie shop in the Norwood Building [with] thirty-somethin' dollars. We bet it on a horse named Dr. Perkins runnin' at Alamo Downs in San Antonio, and he won. Paid about eight to ten to one. . . . Anyhow, we financed Mr. Vosper to the Big Bend with

'racehorse money.' And I got such a kick out of the thing that the first bird dog puppy I named after that I named Dr. Perkins. And he was a good dog.[25]

A search of the NPS and TPWD archives for these watercolor paintings has not been successful.

A Lifelong Partnership

In March 1935, the NPS assigned both Vosper and Stripling to Goliad. Vosper was transferred as a landscape foreman with a recommendation for promotion to superintendent, and both men were to report to the county judge. Judge White and the Texas Centennial Commission had been instrumental in getting funds and a CCC company for the restoration of the Spanish colonial mission Nuestra Señora del Espíritu Santo de Zuñiga.[26] This was a great opportunity for the two men and a number of their friends and even family including sculptor Hugo Villa, former Vosper UT student Temple Phinney, former Vosper A&M student Richard Stewart Colley, Robert Leon White, and Bradley Vosper joined them. NPS records, which

Stripling also saved and that are now part of the Stripling Collection at the Cushing Memorial Library and Archives, show that Vosper started as the supervising architect. According to Stripling, Harold Ickes, then Secretary of the Department of the Interior, switched the roles of the two men so that Stripling became superintendent and Vosper architect. Stripling says,

"It didn't bother him [Vosper] a damn bit. He was glad to be relieved of the duties."[27] Not one to be too interested in paperwork, this arrangement freed Vosper to conduct research on Spanish missions in San Antonio and elsewhere and to concentrate his efforts on what he did best—designing and preparing the architectural drawings.

The Stripling Collection contains numerous photographs that are part of the research that he and Vosper conducted for their design of this custodian's group of structures that includes a dwelling. Care was taken to make use of Spanish-Colonial style indigenous building techniques and design features to relate the structure to the mission. The beautifully drawn plans for this building, dated November 19, 1935, were drawn by Stripling and "recommended" by Vosper. The Stripling Collection also includes numerous photographs of the completed project, suggesting the two men were satisfied with their design, including the undated image at left. The image below was taken in 2016. (Courtesy of Cushing Memorial Library and Archives, Texas A&M University)

The restoration of the mission was complex, involving extensive historic research and in-situ investigations to conclude the proper reconstruction decisions, and would take until 1941 to complete. A team consisting of archeologists, landscape architects, architects, stone masons, and historians worked together to discover, to the best of their ability, the original appearance of the mission. Beaux-Arts-trained architects would be familiar with archeology, documentation of historic artifacts, and architectural history—all tools for restoration—and were encouraged to "put themselves into the past" in order to understand the essence of the classical period of architectural design. In these nascent years of historic preservation in the United States, reconstructions of lost historic sites and features were undertaken with less concern for actual documentation than is the case today. Yet, the NPS was already providing guidance for preservation practice. The Stripling Collection includes a document titled "Conservation of State Historic and Archeological Sites" that reads like a precursor to the 1976 *Secretary of the Interior's Standards for the Treatment of Historic Properties*, today's guiding document.

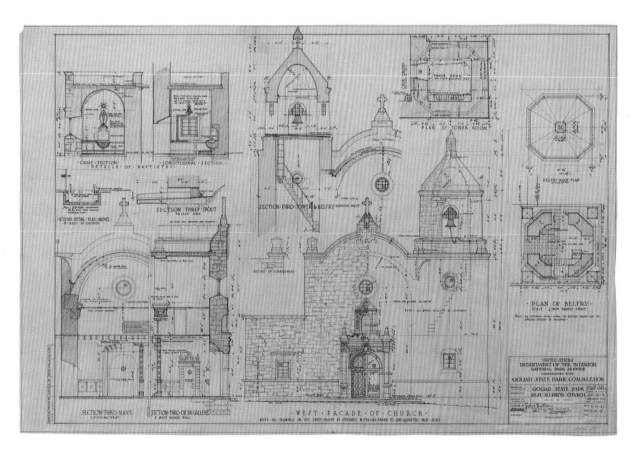

This drawing for the restoration of the mission, prepared by Vosper and checked by Stripling, is dated September 20, 1937—more than two years after the men were assigned to Goliad. The window shown on this drawing of the west façade of the church was repeated as an octagon in Vosper's design for the Goliad Memorial Auditorium on a site directly across Park Road 6, a nod to the new building's context of a couple of centuries earlier. (Courtesy of Goliad State Park, Texas State Parks Board Civilian Conservation Corps drawings, Archives and Information Services Division, Texas State Library and Archives Commission)

This view taken in 2016 is of the west-facing elevation of the mission.

This photograph is believed to have been taken in Goliad and depicts the team of people involved in the restoration of the mission, and possibly other projects in Goliad. Vosper is in the back row, fifth from the right, and Stripling is fifth from the left. There is no date or location on this photograph, which is part of the Raiford Leak Stripling Collection. (Courtesy of Cushing Memorial Library and Archives, Texas A&M University)

When Vosper and Stripling were also commissioned to design the Goliad Memorial Auditorium, the men formed a partnership initially under the name of Vosper & Stripling Architects, which was later changed to S C P Vosper Raiford L. Stripling Associated Architects of Goliad, Texas. The student-mentor relationship had evolved to the point that they could be business partners despite a twenty-five-year age gap and Stripling's relative lack of experience. One of the firm's first projects was this auditorium building, completed in 1937 and designed for the Centennial Division of the Texas State Board of Control, an interesting amalgam of Vosper's work at A&M and the architecture of the mission across the street from it. The design combines plenty of iconography and written words related to Texas' and the region's history with subtler references to the design of the mission. The building has two faces. The front or street face is a wall, with few windows. Opposite that is an open-air corral, where the stepped seating is integrated into the back wall of the auditorium. The corral is completely hidden and comes as

The front façade is entirely made of concrete and features three large panels with written descriptions about the mission and the Presidio La Bahia nearby. The simple white form and the octagonal windows reflect the design of the mission.

The entrance is the only place where ornament is found on this otherwise simple façade, another nod to the Spanish-Colonial style. Hugo Villa, with whom Vosper worked at A&M, sculpted the cast ornament, but instead of casting in molds that would be applied to the face of the building as they were at A&M, here the casting is integral with the concrete that constitutes the primary façade material. This novel approach provided excellent results that remain in good condition today.

a surprise when walking around the outside of the building. On the interior are many of the same materials used at A&M, including a colorful Mexican tile floor, ornamental ironwork, stained-glass light fixtures, cast plaster column capitals with cow heads, a large stage decorated by cast plaster ornament with animal heads and the six flags that flew over Texas. The building was listed on the National Register of Historic Places as a part of the Goliad State Park Historic District in 2001.

Next door is another of the firm's projects for the Texas Centennial, the Fannin Memorial Monument State Park, now Fannin Battleground State Historic Site, completed about 1937. The park features a memorial designed by architect Donald Nelson with sculptor Raoul Josset, both of whom also worked together on the Texas Centennial Exposition in Dallas. All three of the projects in Goliad were part of the promotion of the Texas Centennial in 1936 for which small celebrations were commissioned across the state to coincide with the main event in Dallas.

Vosper left Goliad before the mission project was entirely finished. He suffered the misfortune of losing three family members in the latter part of the 1930s, including his eldest brother John T., who died in 1936, and his brother William A. and his sister Elizabeth M., who both died in 1939. Around 1940, Vosper moved to Washington, DC, to work for the Treasury Department, where he worked in the Procurement Division of that agency. The 1940 US Census lists Vosper as a lodger, divorced, and as having been born in Texas; only the first of those attributes was correct, but it may say something about his sentiments. His wife would move back to New Jersey with their daughter during World War II, and son Bradley, who lived in Goliad at least through 1939, would stay in Texas. In 1942, Vosper again arranged for a job for his old friend Stripling at the BuDocks section of the Washington Navy Yard. After funding for the mission halted due to the war, Stripling left Goliad and moved to Washington, where the two were able to reunite, if briefly. McCullar's book includes a photograph taken by Stripling in 1944 while in Washington, DC, of a smiling Vosper with a birthday cake. On Christmas Day 1945, they moved back to Goliad together, with the intent to pick up where they left off. However, things had changed, and Goliad was just another small, quiet Texas town without much opportunity for an architect.

In search of work, Vosper headed next to Bryan to help Philip G. Norton, his former colleague from the college architect's office at A&M, while Stripling stuck it out another year in Goliad before returning to his hometown of San Augustine to set up a private practice. Vosper lived in the Bryan Hotel in 1946 while working on the design of what remains the tallest structure in downtown Bryan, the Varisco Building, completed in 1948. Described by architectural historian Stephen Fox as a "mini-skyscraper," the design combines Moderne-style characteristics with Modern Movement treatments. Never one to leave out color, Vosper incorporated a blue-green spandrel panel that was a popular material at the time. However, Vosper soon moved on once again, this time to Pampa, Texas, to work with another A&M friend and architect, Royall Cantrell. Stripling drove him back to San Antonio and Cameron's office by 1951.

Vosper's son, Bradley, who had enlisted in the army after one year of college in 1942, graduated from UT in architecture and also moved to Pampa to work with Cantrell, but stayed there. After his father suffered more than one stroke in San Antonio, Bradley moved him back to Pampa in 1956 to keep an eye on his health.

On February 10, 1958, Vosper died of pneumonia in a Pampa hospital at age 71. He was buried at the Fairview Cemetery in Pampa. Bradley would die in Amarillo in 2007, and his sister Janice Gracel (married name Peterson) died in Somerset, New Jersey, in 1995. Augusta died at almost 90 years of age, outliving her husband by 22 years, in New Jersey in 1980.

Vosper-Designed Buildings in Texas

With few buildings credited directly to Vosper, the complete scope of his work in Texas is difficult to ascertain. Credit for his designs come from a number of sources including Vosper's own résumé, newspaper accounts, Vosper's name on drawings, and the recollections of those who knew him such as Stripling. A list of buildings that Vosper has made a significant contribution to as designer from these sources is provided in an appendix.

The legacy at A&M under Giesecke as college architect is very well documented however. Not only are there personal accounts of Vosper's role but his initials are on many of the drawings, usually in the "drawn by" column where the designer would have been recorded. Ernest Langford and others who have taken the time to record the history of the campus' architectural legacy also document his role. A testament to the quality of these buildings is the fact that all ten of them are still in use—even the horse barn. Much of Vosper's work outside of A&M, often listed on the National Register of Historic Places or designated as local landmarks, has been recognized for its value to the built environment. The ten buildings at A&M are less well known but equally qualified for recognition.

3

Vosper at the College

WHEN S. C. P. Vosper joined the college architect's staff in 1929 as chief designer, he brought with him twenty years of experience steeped in Beaux-Arts doctrine, having been educated in this method of design and having taught it to others. He applied the principles of this system but incorporated a modest and more restrained approach that was being adopted by many architects during the period, with references to Texas, Texas history, and the agricultural and mechanical theme of the college, which made his designs uniquely suited for the A&M campus.

The Beaux-Arts Tradition

Vosper's work on the A&M campus is based on his education and practice of the Beaux-Arts tradition in architecture in the United States, which was influenced by the *Ecole des Beaux-Arts* teaching methods and principles founded on classical architecture as precedent for design and in practice from about 1890–1920.[1] Privileged American architects began attending the *Ecole* in Paris in the latter half of the nineteenth century,

bringing back with them a preference for the architecture of ancient Greece, Rome, and the Italian Renaissance, itself a resurrection of these earlier periods of architecture. Interest in classical architecture gained national attention when the "White City" was presented at the Chicago Columbian Exposition of 1893, a world's fair. The exposition was designed as a cohesive ensemble of buildings, all in the same Beaux-Arts style and all painted white. The effect of this group of buildings emphasized the idea that instead of designing one building at a time to be magnificent, one could design buildings as a collection, as in a city, and amplify their impact. The effect was monumental and European—things America aspired to be. The tenets of *Ecole des Beaux-Arts* training would dominate American architectural education for the next thirty or forty years with its emphasis on the study and documentation of classical architecture and on the making of cities. Complementing the architecture were the Beaux-Arts planning principles for grand boulevards, public squares, and civic art known as the "City Beautiful Movement."[2]

The ideas that formed the Beaux-Arts tradition in architecture and planning were disseminated through a system called the *"atelier"* that took hold in schools of architecture, in larger cities that could support these architectural clubs, and even within the larger architectural practices. The purpose of the *atelier* was to provide a place for serious architects to refine their craft under the leadership of an experienced architect, preferably *Ecole*-trained, and to have the potential to earn recognition of their talent. The *atelier* conducted competitions consisting of "problems" or *projets* that were then judged and presented in publications and exhibitions. A grand prize, known as the "Paris Prize," was sought through this process. These clubs and programs within architectural firms were also places for socializing. The Beaux-Arts Society of America, which after 1916 transferred this responsibility to the Beaux-Arts Institute of Design, judged the competition entries, organized the *atelier*, and published their work. As established in the previous chapter, Vosper was firmly rooted in this system through his participation in the *atelier* system as a *Massier* in New York and again in Dallas, and his teaching in the architecture departments at the University of Texas (UT) and the Agricultural and Mechanical (A&M) College of Texas. In these roles, Vosper had a tremendous influence on the next generation of architects in Texas.

The teaching of the Beaux-Arts tradition led to the designation of a Beaux-Arts style, which is reserved for very opulent, monumental and "high style" architecture of the period that is heavily treated with art and ornament. Examples of this style include the US Custom House in New York City, designed by Cass Gilbert in 1907, and Grand Central Station designed by Reed and Stem, Warren and Wetmore in 1913.

The 1920s, although architectural interest in the Beaux-Arts style remained strong, Neo-Classical was also a period of revival styles that included Romanesque Revival, Gothic Revival, Neo-classical, even National Park Service Rustic, all styles that Vosper used. At the same time, architects were moving toward a more modern and geometric interpretation of classicism known as the Moderne and Art Deco styles. Art Deco design was popular in the 1930s, concurrent with Moderne, and subsets of this term such as Streamlined Moderne, Art Moderne, Federal Moderne,

Stripped Classicism, and PWA Moderne, were later defined by architectural historians.[3] The Moderne style eliminated the opulence that typified the Beaux-Arts style. The paring down of these styles and the more restrained use of ornament was particularly appropriate at the peak of their popularity during the Great Depression. This interest in historical styles and in ornament came to a halt in the late 1930s after Walter Gropius and Ludwig Mies van der Rohe brought the ideas of the Bauhaus school into architectural pedagogical circles.

Vosper was a man of his time and had learned his craft very well. With respect to style at the A&M College of Texas, his designs can be best classified as Moderne, Classical Moderne, and PWA Moderne (or WPA Moderne, standing respectively for Public Works Administration or Works Progress Administration, a reference to the time period during which this style was most common) styles. Vosper's use of ornament was atypical for the Moderne and PWA Moderne style—he used a little bit more than would have been conventional for this style. Some of his ornament is highly characteristic of the Art Deco style. The extra ornamentation may be attributed to his background with both the Beaux-Arts tradition and possibly his experience designing theaters, or perhaps it was a personal predilection. In other respects, however, including massing, symmetry, simpler materials, and steel windows, the A&M buildings reflect the characteristic of the PWA Moderne and Classical Moderne styles, an appropriate choice for college buildings, and a popular style from the early 1930s until World War II.

One of the strengths of architects during this period was their ability to design in any style, as opposed to having a distinctive style of their own. The personal style of an architect could be found in the details, and young architects were trained to follow the rules and to contribute to a larger whole rather than personal expression. This emphasis on the collective impact of building, whether in cities or on campuses, is something Vosper subscribed to, as evidenced by his choice of PWA Moderne, which is rooted in the Beaux-Arts style that was used on the A&M campus prior to his arrival. He also chose a similar colored brick and cast stone as the primary materials for the exterior, the predominant materials on campus at that time. Likewise, his buildings are of a similar scale at typically three stories high.

At the same time, Vosper brought his own set of consistent material choices, color palette, and details that identify his group of buildings as his. Here are some of the concepts, typically also tenets of the Beaux-Arts tradition, that Vosper creatively incorporated into the buildings at A&M:

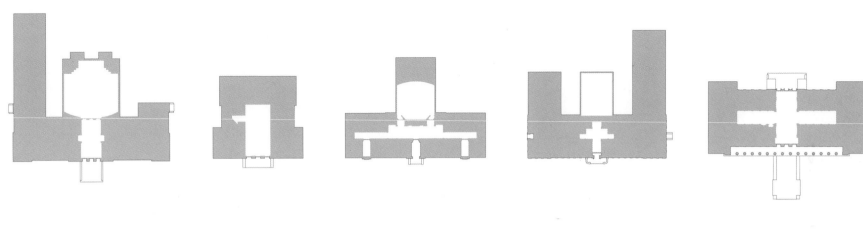

The parti

The *parti* is the French term for the organizational idea of the plan. Here are plan diagrams for the seven academic buildings that illustrate the similarities in their *parti*. In each of the five buildings with a lecture room, the room is expressed as a separate volume, either attached at the back or sandwiched in the middle of two wings. At the Chemistry, Petroleum, and Veterinary Hospital Buildings, the lecture room is attached at the center of the back, expressed as an important two-story volume of space. At the Agricultural Engineering and Animal Industries Buildings, the lecture room is expressed as a two-story volume between a front wing and a back wing. The front wing serves the academic side of education, while the back wing serves the practice side, with the lecture room placed in the middle as a symbolic gesture for where these two facets of education come together. The entrance is always in the center of the façade, which is always symmetrical. The essential circulation patterns in these diagrams also illustrate the way in which people move through a series of steps, porches and spaces toward the most important space, be it a lecture room, reading room, or reception space. (Courtesy of Quimby McCoy Preservation Architecture, LLP)

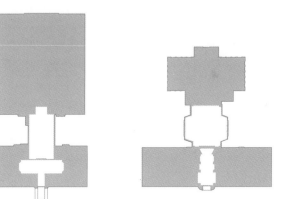

The piano nobile

The *piano nobile*, an Italian term meaning "noble floor," is typically the floor of the building with the most important spaces or purpose. The idea relates to an urban building like a *palazzo* where the ground floor would be the noisiest and least private level and the first floor, raised above the street, would be the most desirable. Above the first floor, there might be other floors, and at the top floor would be an attic story, the least desirable due to its access by stairs. In classical architecture, the ground floor level is related to the *podium*, a raised pedestal or base that elevates the building off the ground and creates the opportunity for an attenuated entrance experience, typically with a grand stair. This idea is found in some form on all of Vosper's buildings. The podium is typically expressed with a different material such as a cast stone water table or may incorporate a basement or ground floor level. There is always a grand stair or a porch element in front of the entrance. The Administration Building demonstrates this concept in its purest form with a full ground floor designated in a darker color of cast stone and a grand stair leading to a two-story high loggia that expresses the two most important floors of the building topped by a third floor that acts as an attic story of lesser importance.

Hierarchy

The use of a *piano nobile* establishes the hierarchy of the floors within the building. The concept of expressing the relative importance of the various parts of the building through adherence to rules of architectural design such as symmetry, axis, scale, and the choice of the column order is a characteristic found in Vosper's buildings. Hierarchy is a concept employed at the scale of the city or campus down to the scale of ornament. On the A&M campus, the Administration Building is placed facing the entrance and on a primary axis in the campus plan to signify its importance, while the academic discipline buildings face interior quadrangles or streets. The classical order for the Administration Building columns is the Ionic order, which signifies importance but not opulence or grandiosity. On the front of the building, the column and its capital are expressed in the round while on the back, campus side the column is integrated in the wall as a pilaster with a more two-dimensional capital. Hierarchy is further expressed with the choice of the lion as the animal head adorning the cornice and in the more accurate use of classical language that is found on this building.

The expression of hierarchy is also found in the processional experience of entering the building, starting with the appearance of the exterior, where the entrance is always in the center and the most prominent feature of the façade, through ante-spaces such as a grand stair, then porches or a loggia, and finally inside the building, where the procession continues until the most important space is reached.

Architecture Parlante

Architecture parlante is the ability of architecture to "speak" to the visitor. In Vosper's buildings, this is accomplished in several ways. Actual words are used either directly by spelling out the name of the building, as on the Administration Building, or as poems or adages carved into panels or steps to provide a clue as to its purpose, as on the Chemistry Building. Another device for "speaking" is the use of a shield or *cartouche* above the entrance that includes symbolism pertaining to the purpose. Decorative panels with allegorical content or symbolism are used as decoration near entrances or in a spandrel panel located beneath and between windows. At the smallest scale, the ornament provides an opportunity for further communication. This idea is also found in the interior decoration. With Vosper, these are also opportunities for a wink or witty commentary that is slipped in unexpectedly and can easily be overlooked. *Architecture parlante*, more than any other design component, makes the buildings endearing and memorable.

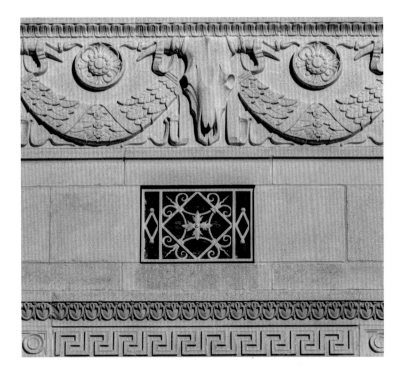

Polychromy

Polychromy, meaning the artful use of multiple colors in the decoration of a building or object, is typically subtle color introduced at selective areas of the building in Beaux-Arts style architecture. The Administration Building and Cushing Library are examples of the more subtle color integration that was expected of the Beaux-Arts style. Vosper took the use of color to another level with the WPA Moderne style, where he used distinctive patterned and colorful Mexican tiles on the façades and as paving material. The use of color in the decoration of interiors is also part of Vosper's repertoire, carefully coordinated between the exterior and interior of the building.

Agrafes

Agrafes is a method of linking one architectural ornament to another. The term literally means "link" in French and is also used to describe a decorated keystone that connects the stone *voussoir* in an arch. In Beaux-Arts design, the art of *agrafes* is in the ability to link traditional classical ornament, such as dentils or the egg-and-dart molding, to other ornament that may be part of the architect's expression of the building's purpose. Vosper was particularly adept at incorporating all manner of live, dead, human, animal, plant, and insect features—just about anything you can imagine—into traditional moldings and forms to create a seamless treatment where nothing appears out of place.

Crafted materials

The materials with which Vosper achieved his design are often dependent on a craftsman, whether for the creation of sculptural cast stone or for decorative painting. Craftsmen were readily available during this period, when they were an integrated part of the building process of revival-style architecture. Vosper had come to know many of the best craftsmen in Texas through his work in Austin and San Antonio, and he drew heavily on those contacts while at A&M. The Great Depression encouraged the use of manual labor and hand-made materials as a way to put more people to work. This component of the Vosper buildings is unlikely to be reproduced as the circumstances that made it possible will not be repeated.

Art and architecture integration

The integration of art and architecture is one of the most important tenets of Beaux-Arts architecture and of the City Beautiful Movement, which often encouraged the design of monumental public buildings and spaces heavily adorned with sculpture. In Vosper's designs, the sculptural component is found in other forms of ornament that is fully integrated into the architectural elements of the building, such as entrance surrounds, string and belt courses, pediments, and entablatures. The ornament, which can be very three-dimensional, as in the animal heads at the top of the Veterinary Hospital Building or the *anthemion* ornament that runs along the top of the Administration Building, is the art in Vosper's designs. So are the panels of relief, sometimes with allegorical content, that are used as decoration on the façades. Finally, there may also be artwork integrated into the design of the interior such as the relief panels within doorway pediments.

Materials

Vosper used a limited palette of materials. One set of architectural specifications can be found in the Cushing Memorial Library and Archives with the contract papers for the Animal Industries Building. This is a standard specification that Vosper edited for each project and will be a valuable resource for any future restoration and repair work. The following is a list of the predominant materials found on Vosper's buildings.

In the photographic essays on the ten buildings that follow this chapter, examples of these concepts and the use of these materials will be exposed little by little until by the end of the last building—the Animal Industries Building—there will be a sense of what these designs were all about, what to cherish about them, and hopefully what memories will come with seeing them again, possibly again for the first time.

Exterior Materials:

Brick, wire cut

Cast stone

Ornamental ironwork

Mexican cement tile

Steel windows

Stained and leaded glass

Interior Materials:

Plaster

Cast plaster

Marble

Glazed hollow clay tile

Mexican cement tile

Terrazzo

Ceramic tile

Composition floor tile

Acoustical ceiling tile

Stained and leaded glass

Patterned glass

Ornamental ironwork

Wood doors, windows, and cabinetry

Russialoid-wrapped wood doors

This map shows the location of Vosper's ten buildings on the campus. It is somewhat remarkable that all ten of them have survived on a campus that is continually changing and growing—a testament to their value perhaps. (Courtesy of Quimby McCoy Preservation Architecture, LLP)

4

The Chemistry Building

    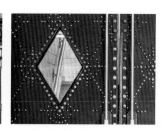

DATE COMPLETED: 1929 (phase 1); 1933 (phase 2)

COST: $95,000 (phase 1); $401,853.97 (phase 2)

ARCHITECT: F. E. Giesecke [Phillip G. Norton (phase 1); S. C. P. Vosper (phase 2)]

CONTRACTOR: W. A. Orth, construction superintendent,
A&M College of Texas (phase 1); unknown (phase 2)

"Magnificent."

—Stephen Hawking, remark upon seeing the lecture room in the Chemistry
Building where he gave a talk on April 27, 1995.[1]

THE FIRST phase of the building may not have benefited from Vosper's input, but the second phase made up for it. This is one of three of the seven academic buildings to have retained its original use. The continuity of use and the dedication of a long-time building proctor, Assistant Department Head Ronald G. Carter '74, are two reasons that this building is one of the best preserved on campus.

History

Built on the site of the varsity tennis courts, the Chemistry Building replaced an earlier department facility known as "King Chem" and as the "VetChem" building because it was shared with veterinary medicine. When Vosper arrived at the college in late 1929, the first "emergency" phase of the building was already constructed. The emergency was the need to quickly construct a new chemistry building in order to demolish the old one so that the library could be constructed on the site. Since Vosper came to befriend Philip G. Norton, the designer for this

phase, and the two men got along well according to accounts of the Cushing Library construction, it can be surmised that Vosper liked Norton's handsome design. This phase, the north wing of the building today, features a polychromatic terra-cotta cornice and an interesting green terra-cotta screen element under the windows to conceal the ventilation system for the laboratories. The second phase, which includes the front and west main body of the building with the central lecture room wing, was completed in 1933 and includes all of Vosper's trademark design choices, elegantly transitioned from the design of the earlier wing at a side entrance on Ross Street.

The total funding for the building came to approximately $500,000. During this same period, Rice University built a Chemistry Building for approximately $1 million and the University of Texas (UT) spent approximately $800,000 on its Chemistry Building, now known as Welch Hall and completed in 1931. The design of the decoration in Welch Hall's lecture room and library, which was designed by Greene LaRoche & Dahl (the successor firm to Herbert Greene Company for whom Vosper worked soon

A color photograph taken in 1939 has faded considerably but depicts the Chemistry Building as it would have appeared soon after completion in 1933. The landscape shown here is typical of the type of planting that was used for this building program, with funding established in 1931 to implement Fritz Hensel's "beautification plans." The style of the landscape is so consistent that it is possible to date photographs by the planting alone. The street in the foreground is Ireland Street, which now dead-ends at Ross Street and has been replaced by a plaza featuring a large fountain. (Courtesy of Cushing Memorial Library and Archives, Texas A&M University)

after his arrival in Dallas) working with Robert Leon White as the UT supervising architect, features ornate ceilings, chemical symbolism, stained glass, and ornamental ironwork. All three chemistry buildings are impressive and have an abundance of decoration.

The first significant addition to the building was completed about 1959, and this expansion finished the south wing of the earlier design to form an E-shaped building. Designed to harmonize with the existing building, this addition used materials and details that are simpler but very similar to those in the 1933 structure, an approach that was often utilized by the campus architect in the 1950s. In later decades, this approach was abandoned in favor of interventions that stood out, sometimes in stark contrast to what already existed. A 1972 annex to the building that connects to the south wing demonstrates this approach. The last addition to what by now was called the Chemistry Complex included 116,000 square feet at a cost of $15.5 million, designed by the architectural firm of Pierce Goodwin Alexander of Houston and completed in 1987. That building, fronting on Ross Street, is designed in a contemporary style and is not a physical addition to the original building at all. This new building was followed by an interior renovation of the original building at a cost of $7 million in 1993. This renovation took four years to complete and two contractors, but the end result maintained all the exterior and updated the interior without sacrificing any of the historic character. The approach to this renovation was to keep as many of the original walls and materials as possible, in part to save money, resulting in a well-preserved interior that complements the exterior.

Description

At four stories, including a basement that is barely below ground, the Chemistry Building departs only slightly from classical traditions in the height and arrangement of its floors. Instead of the first floor—*piano-nobile*—being the tallest of the floors, here it is the same height as the upper stories, while the basement story is shorter. The basement, or base of the building, is differentiated by the use of a pink-brown cast stone instead of brick. At each end of the base are inscriptions carved in stone: on the left side, from Aristotle, is "Let us first understand the facts, and then we may see the cause." On the right side, from J. Von Liebig, is "The secret of all who make discoveries is to look upon nothing as impossible."

The entrance is emphasized by a grand stair that ascends almost the entire basement story. The stair leads to three entrance doors, each surrounded by cast stone classical pediments, in a golden-tan cast stone that complements the brick. The brick facades are accented with more cast stone and vertical bands of windows, separated by Mexican tile panels known as spandrel panels. The original steel casement windows have been replaced by aluminum windows, part of a campus-wide window replacement program in the 1980s. At the top of the building is an attic story featuring ironwork grills and cast stone plaques. The style of the building is PWA Moderne. The materials here include the full palette that was used on Vosper's academic buildings, including buff brick, cast stone, colorful Mexican tile, ornamental metal, and stained glass.

The form of the building is an E with the central leg serving as the lecture room. The other two wings house laboratories and classrooms as well as administrative spaces on the first floor and basement level. This simple arrangement of the building creates two courtyards that serve to provide light and air to the interior spaces. The symmetry of the plan is reflected in the facades and creates a circulation pattern that always returns to both the lecture room, the symbolic and actual center of the building, and the entrance.

The lobby provides immediate clues about the quality and character of this building's interior. The dramatic and modern effect of the glossy black pigmented structural glass walls and gold ornamental plaster sets the tone. The floor combines black and gray marble with inset colorful Mexican tile in green and with a border of patterned tile. The ceiling features heavily ornamented plaster medallions, set off with gold. Built-in display cases provide a place for showcasing the work of the department. Front and center is an elaborate and dramatic staircase that leads to the *piece de resistance*—the lecture room.

The diagram near right depicts the plan organization of the building—the *parti*—with emphasis on the public and most important spaces which lead to the lecture room. The diagram on the far right illustrates the vertical arrangement of these same spaces, starting outside the building and into the lecture room. (Courtesy of Quimby McCoy Preservation Architecture, LLP)

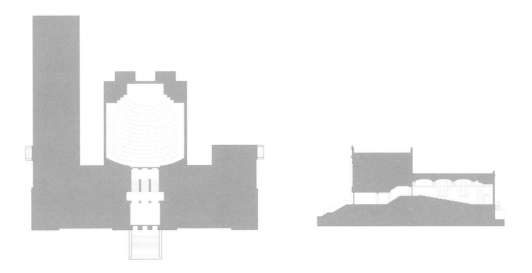

The experience at all of Vosper's buildings begins with a special and colorful cement tile at the entrance landing, except at the Administration Building where the tile is patterned but gray. Here, the gold and dark red (maroon) colors in the tile are echoed in the golden-tan color of the cast stone and again in the colorful Mexican tile on the façade. The landing tiles were recently replaced with replicas of the original tiles, made in Mexico. The original tiles were removed in 1994, reportedly because the old ones were slippery when wet and created a safety hazard, requiring new slip-resistant gray tile. The new gray ones were slip resistant, as reported by the *Battalion*. Apparently the slip-resistant gray tile was in need of replacement in 2016 when a restoration of this feature prevailed. The original tile has survived in front of the entrances of nearly all of the other Vosper buildings.

Vosper typically placed a cast stone cartouche, or shield, over the entrance to identify the purpose of the building without spelling out the actual name, an example of *architecture parlante*. In some cases, the shield is augmented by a logo, also designed by Vosper. These buildings are likely the only place one would find this shield or logo, as they are not official emblems of the college or department, but they do create an attractive object of interest. Here there are matching shields on the attic story of the bays that flank the entrance. Each shield is divided into four parts, interpreted loosely here as (from top left clockwise): art, represented by a painter's palette; academics, represented by a globe, scales, book, and pen; agriculture, represented by a sickle and a wheat stalk; and mechanics by a gear and plow. At the center is a smaller shield depicting the symbol for unity and balance—a combination of the four elements of earth, air, fire, and water. Like much of the iconography and symbolism used by Vosper, this decorative element is also just a part of the architectural composition, a blend of classical ornament and stylized elements that do not always make perfect sense but are in the spirit of the thing. Above the shield are alternating sizes of the classical *anthemion*, and below are owls' heads, a symbol of wisdom.

Symbols for the elements are also used within each of the panels that separate windows, called spandrels, that are decorated with colorful Mexican tile in green, maroon, gold, and pale blue. The chevron pattern of alternating colors flanking the center cast stone relief panel is a popular pattern found in PWA Moderne and Art Deco design. The symbol shown (*left*) is for "earth." On the bays flanking the entrance, the single symbols are replaced by a more ornate cast stone relief panel (*right*), featuring what appears to be a stylized burning Bunsen burner heating something with smoke, if the ornament can be taken literally.

Many of Vosper's buildings still have their original light fixtures, like this example featuring stained and patterned glass with ornamental ironwork. Note the white metal with perforations depicting symbols for earth, moon, and unity/balance at the top of the fixture. The gold-colored glass complements the warm golden tones of the cast stone and tile.

Stylized classical ornament of the Ionic order continues from the exterior into the lobby and lecture room. The lobby is dramatic, with a faintly Egyptian character, sporting highly reflective black *Carrara* glass walls (a brand of pigmented structural glass that enjoyed a short but notable period of popularity in the 1930s, particularly on Moderne and Art Deco style buildings) and contrasting aluminum and gold-painted display cases and light fixtures, along with gold-painted cast plaster ornament on the ceiling and at column capitals. This carefully preserved space is one of the most impressive on the campus. Today the ceiling is painted white, no doubt to bring some light into the space, but originally it would have had a darker, glazed, and stippled finish.

Each of Vosper's lobbies includes space for the display of the user's academic field of study. The aluminum trim and moldings surrounding the display cases are given a faux-painted finish to mimic bronze, a technique used in several of the buildings on ironwork and even wood, presumably to save some money. The Ionic order continues to be stylized here above the central display case, as it is in the ceiling.

The interior and exterior light fixtures are designed for this collection of buildings and, like some of the cast plaster ornament, are repeated among the buildings yet seem perfectly suited to each. While the plaster ornament in this image is only found in this building, the light fixture was used in the Agricultural Engineering and the Geology and Petroleum Engineering Buildings. An artisan and foundry such as Voss Metals or Alamo Metals would have manufactured this type of custom fixture. There is also a highly decorative cast plaster ceiling medallion in the lobby, but outside of this image, that is repeated in the lecture room of the Agricultural Engineering Building. Despite reusing plaster molds, light fixtures, and other elements, each of the buildings gives the impression that the decoration is unique and purposefully designed for its place.

Stairs are a special opportunity for dramatic effect and an important circulation feature for any building. With a complex arrangement of steps going up and down with multiple colors of terrazzo; ornamental iron railings; patterned Mexican tile walls and floors in gold, green, and dark red colors; brown glazed tile wainscoting; and groin vaulted ceilings, there are many repeated forms, colors, materials, and patterns that make the use of these stairs a magical experience. From the lobby, the stairs in the center go down to a landing (*left*) from which one can turn left or right and then continue further down to the basement level of the building (*right*). The stairs to each side of the center stair go up to a midlevel landing from which is entered the lecture room. From that midlevel landing are stairs that lead to the second floor. Note the star-shaped pendant light fixture, part of a family of aluminum and glass fixtures used in the building.

The intricate hammered-finish ironwork of the stair railing is typical of the craftsmanship that was not only possible but encouraged during the Depression. Elegantly detailed, hand-wrought iron like this provided work for an underemployed population. At the same time, the craft of working with materials was still a largely family-run skill, handed down by generation, which was available and well known to Vosper from his work in larger cities like San Antonio, Dallas, and Austin. The relationship between architects and craftsmen was an important one: these were the people with the skill to make an architect's design become reality. Vosper, like other architects of his day, had long-term business relationships with a variety of craftspeople and brought several of these to College Station, including Alamo Metals and Voss Metals, both of San Antonio. However, as important as the skill of making this ornamental metal was and still is, the design of this railing was completely determined by a drawing prepared by Vosper. In this case, the drawing is scaled at ½ inch per foot, but sometimes Vosper would draw ornaments or other elements full size to hand to the craftsman who would make it. Here, one can compare the finished product on the left with the architect's drawing below. Vosper designed each of the buildings to this level of detail, an astounding feat when considering the time frame during which all of this design and construction work was accomplished. (Copyright 2016 Texas A&M University)

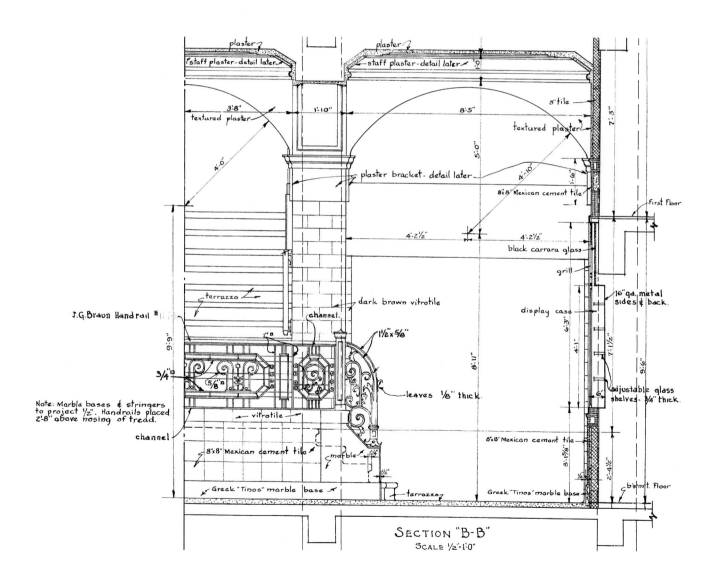

SECTION "B-B"
SCALE ½"=1'-0"

You would never know it by the way the room looks today, but in 1952 the campus' most magnificent lecture room was seriously compromised when for a sum of $439.00 and ten days' work the room was repainted in one color, "to be selected by College Architect," from the "mould to ceiling down to base."[2] While it is hard to imagine why this made sense at the time, the same thing occurred at the Agricultural Engineering and Animal Industries Buildings, and possibly others. What color, you might ask? Institutional Green!

It is not known how long the room remained green, and long-time faculty members do not remember it, but we do know that in 1992 the room was generally restored to its original appearance. This classroom, which can be used by the entire university today, and this building were the first of the Vosper-era interiors to be celebrated. More recently, the lecture room of the Agricultural Engineering Building was restored, and the Petroleum Engineering and Geology Building is scheduled for a similar treatment. The Classroom Improvement Committee, chaired by chemistry's Ronald Carter, oversees the improvements to these classrooms. Improvements typically include new audio-visual equipment, carpeting, seating, and blackout shades. However, as is evident in this classroom, the Committee is also concerned with taking into consideration the unique architectural character and materials that survive, making it possible for Aggies to enjoy these spaces now and in the future.[3] The Chemistry lecture room is possibly the most beautiful room of its type on campus. The combination of historic features like the long black chalkboard, steep stepped seating, elaborate plaster moldings and decoration, and the dramatic effect of the gold painted finishes are very effective. Note the stepped wall treatment at the stage, at left, and the way the horizontal bands of the ceiling decoration run into the sides of the windows at each end of the room, below.

Special details like this stylized Ionic-order pilaster capital adorned with the traditional *anthemion*, or honeysuckle ornament, that also supports a light fixture have been restored with a gold paint finish that is a feature of the decorative painting scheme in the lecture room. The gold paint is the predominant finish in the room, but there are smaller moldings that are accented in colors that include a blue-green, a dark red, and silver. If these finishes were similar to those in Vosper's other buildings, these paints may have been glazed to achieve a mottled or stippled effect that provides depth and an "old world" appearance, possibly with areas of the glaze wiped off to expose the brighter color below.

The use of gold paint is a common substitute for gold leaf. Often, the substitute paint would utilize bronze powder to achieve its gold appearance. There are hundreds of different shades and particle sizes available in bronze powders; most have a small amount of zinc, copper, and aluminum alloys. This type of paint is known to have been used at the Agricultural Engineering Building, for which a detailed historic finishes study was prepared. Over time, the bronze powder paint will oxidize to a brownish-green color, like bronze, which spoils its effect. However, modern-day gold paint can utilize more stable pigments and gold powder for a similar effect. Glazing was often used on top of the gold paint, where it may have been wiped away in certain areas to create highlights. The rest of the ceiling and wall surfaces appear in historic photographs to have been also glazed, which would have made the room much darker than it is today. However, the lecture rooms and other spaces in the building must function and be practical to maintain. For this reason, no walls and only a few ceilings with the original dark finish remain in Vosper's buildings, suggesting that this treatment was not the most practical for a university setting.

This historic photograph was taken before 1952 and shows the room with the original dark walls and ceilings. As beautiful as the room is today, it is hard to imagine what the space must have been like in person with the significantly darker wall and ceiling finishes. The original wood desks and just about everything else in this photograph are still in use. (Courtesy of Cushing Memorial Library and Archives, Texas A&M University)

The doors to this room are made of wood covered with Russialoid, imitation leather manufactured by Pantasote Company of New York that is similar to the better-known brand Naugahyde, which was expected to last longer than real leather and be easier to clean. The Pantasote Leather Company also claimed its product was fireproof and stain-proof, among other benefits. The material, often misspelled, was used on car and boat upholstery as well as on furniture and doors. Vosper used this for all the lecture room doors in the academic buildings. The doors incorporate brass nails set in a decorative pattern; there are three different patterns in the room. The doors shown here were restored with new matching covering material in 1992.

A geometric pattern in stained glass adorns the windows in the lecture room. In 1933, these windows would have been operable and an important means of ventilation, as well as natural light. Fans, usually wall mounted, would also have been used in the room to create a soft breeze. The colors in the stained glass are the same colors used on the exterior and interior of the building.

This corridor is typical for Vosper's corridor designs, featuring a glazed tile wainscot in a soft and mottled tan color, terrazzo flooring, wood doors with transom windows, windows—to allow for air-flow through the corridor and into the rooms on each side—and a simple flat plaster ceiling. The finishes for the ceilings are unknown. Light fixtures were most likely "school house" style, but not many historic images exist of spaces like the corridors to confirm this. The Chemistry Building is one of a few of Vosper's buildings to retain its original corridors. In other buildings, these spaces are irreversibly altered with dropped ceilings and the removal of windows and transoms, often the result of air-conditioning installations. The wood display cases were added by the department to complement the original design.

Water fountain

The care that has been taken with the original corridors extends to the smaller details, such as the retention of the original "refrigerated water fountains."

Even some of the original laboratories are still functioning today.

5

The Cushing Library

DATE COMPLETED: September 1930

COST: $225,000, approximately

ARCHITECT: F. E. Giesecke (Philip G. Norton, designer with S. C. P. Vosper)

CONTRACTOR: William A. Orth, construction superintendent,
A&M College of Texas

*"Contrary to general opinion, the A. and M. student body is a reading student body,
men who read to improve their minds, not for mere recreation."*[1]

—The *Bryan Daily Eagle*, 1924

LIKE THE Chemistry Building, Cushing Library has been expanded more times than most buildings on campus. Like the Veterinary Hospital, changes also took a toll on the interior, which was nearly replaced in its entirety, but with restoration in mind so that there remains at least an interpretation of the original design.

History

A library is traditionally the heart of a college, hence the central location of Cushing Library just east of the Academic Building. The building is named after Colonel Edward Benjamin Cushing (1862–1924), class of 1880, who served as president of the college when in 1911–12, both the Mess Hall and Old Main were destroyed by fire. Cushing is also credited with saving the college from financial ruin by writing checks or vouchers from his own accounts when the state legislature could not provide funding quickly enough. The college library was first housed in Old Main in 1879, which was replaced in 1913 with the Aca-

demic Building, which housed the library until the construction of this purpose-built edifice in 1930. Built on the site of the former Chemistry Building (the new Chemistry Building had to be completed before the old one could be demolished for the new library), the library was designed before the campus was reoriented to the east. This explains why its entrance faces west, toward the back of the Academic Building. The design of the library was already complete and the start of construction coincided roughly with Vosper's arrival in College Station.

The history of the library involves one addition after another, each enveloping the building before it. The first addition was actually a separate building at the back of Cushing, built as a memorial to Gibb Gilchrist in 1962 for the Texas Engineering Library. That building was enveloped by the first true addition in 1968, designed first as two stories but finally built as a four-story addition to the rear of the Cushing Library that enlarged the library eight-fold. This addition enclosed the Texas Engineering Library on all sides, including the roof. Later named the Sterling C. Evans Library Complex, it was designed by architect

Cushing Library as it appeared in 1954, before the first of many additions. (Courtesy of Cushing Memorial Library and Archives, Texas A&M University)

Donald Jarvis '49 of Fisher-Jarvis, Putty and Jarvis of Dallas, and portions of this design are visible today. Just a decade later came the next addition, completed in 1979, again to the back of the previous addition. At this stage there was consideration given to demolishing the original building in order to build a high-rise, a plan that was never carried out.[2] Instead, another addition, this time six-stories tall and covering some of its predecessor, was designed by Preston M. Geren, Jr. '45 of Fort Worth, the grandson of Frederick E. Giesecke.

Cushing's interior went through several changes starting with the removal of murals in the lobby sometime after 1946, the installation of air conditioning in 1955, and the most dramatic change that ended up involving the removal and reconstruction of the building's interior in 1996. This last dramatic restoration coincided with the creation of a Special Collections, Manuscripts and Archives unit and the naming of Dr. David Chapman '67 as university archivist. The project was designed by Graeber, Simmons & Cowan AIA Architects of Austin after a complete gutting of the building was deemed necessary for the abatement of asbestos and lead-based paint. This process necessitated the reconstruction of just about everything in the building, including the decorative ceiling in the reading room, the terrazzo flooring, and even the furniture. The building was renamed the Cushing Memorial Library.

Description

Three stories with a basement that is more than half below ground, the facades are arranged with the *piano nobile* at the second floor, rather than at the more traditional first floor, with a higher floor to ceiling height than other floors to express the importance of the reading room that occupies the entire west façade at this level. The basement story is clad in rusticated cast stone while the upper floors are of brick and cast stone with two-story-high pilasters that give the façade its monumentality. The original steel casement windows have been replaced by aluminum. The top of the building is designed with a broad frieze that includes the name of the building. This building is more Neoclassical in its style than most of the other buildings, due in part to Norton's design but also as an expression of hierarchy. The traditional use of classical architectural language is more formal and monumental than the PWA Moderne style used on the Chemistry Building, befitting the importance of a library on the campus. The only other design that is more formal and monumental is the Administration Building.

The form of the building is a subtle H-shape with a larger front (west) wing housing the lobby and reading room connected by a short middle section to a rear (east) wing housing the book stacks. The east wing reflects the regularity of the stacks with smaller windows and more floor levels. The pilaster capitals and cornice are much simpler on the middle and rear wing, appropriately expressing the hierarchy of the spaces within the building.

A short set of steps leads to three entrances with classical pediments that open into the lobby. The lobby is a large open space, described on the architectural drawings as a "Trophy Room," leading to smaller reading rooms, including the "Asbury Browsing Room," where students could gather to smoke and enjoy idle moments, as the *Battalion* described it. On the left side, out of view, was a large staircase leading to the second floor "Charging Room" from which one could enter the stacks on the left or the reading room on the right. On the third floor was the "Music Room," with a modern remote control record player with 1,000 records complete with card index and 300 volumes on music and musicians, donated to the library by the Carnegie Corporation. This simple arrangement of spaces provided the flexibility that enabled the building to adapt more easily to later changes.

The diagram on the left depicts the plan organization of the building—the *parti*—with emphasis on the public and most important spaces that lead to the reading room. The diagram on the right illustrates the vertical arrangement of these same spaces, starting outside the building and into the reading room. (Courtesy of Quimby McCoy Preservation Architecture, LLP)

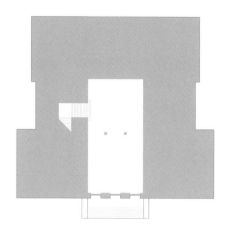

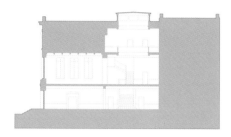

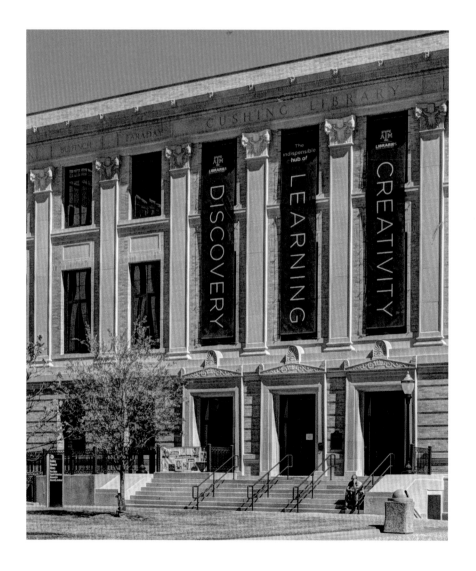

One of the most basic decisions made by the designer of a neoclassical style building is the choice of an order, defined by the style of the column capital, that also prescribes the proportions, moldings, and even ornament that is suitable. The choice of the Ionic order for an academic building is appropriate; this order is reserved for important buildings but is not as ostentatious as the more flamboyant Corinthian or Composite order nor as simple as the Doric or Tuscan order. However, Norton and Vosper do not confine themselves to an entirely accurate representation of the order. Instead, the capitals, which traditionally feature volutes (see the more correct capitals on the Administration Building) are replaced here by rams' heads that flank a *bucranium*, an ox's skull commonly used in classical architecture, with a shield and leaves above. The column capitals and the small owls' heads that are used along the cornice are the only references to creative and referential use of ornament on this otherwise reserved façade.

Each of the three entrances features a flattened pediment like this one, topped with an oversized classical *anthemion*, or honeysuckle ornament, in the center and at both corners. The frieze of the pediment is heavily decorated with plant materials. Beneath the pediment is the classical egg and dart molding.

This drawing of a portion of the façade by Norton illustrates the style of drawing that was promoted by the *Ecole des Beaux-Arts* and that permeated architectural education in the United States. Note the precision with which the column capitals and other details are drawn. (Copyright 2016 Texas A&M University)

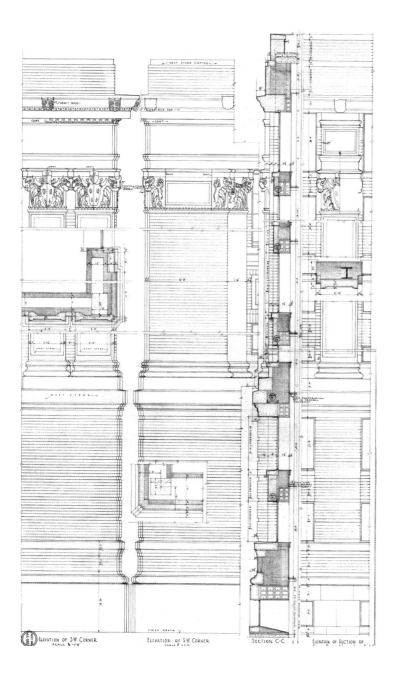

Along the frieze of the entablature near the top of the building, to each side of the building name, are incised the names of important scholars, philosophers, architects, and scientists. The names, selected by a committee of deans, include Austrian botanist Gregor Mendel, founder of genetics; German botanist Julian von Sachs, founder of plant physiology; English essayist and reformer Francis Bacon; US architect Charles Bulfinch; English scientist Michael Faraday, who worked with electricity and magnetism; Scottish physicist James Clerk Maxwell; French chemist and bacteriologist Louis Pasteur; English poet and dramatist William Shakespeare; Greek philosopher Plato; Scottish steam engine developer James Watt; English mathematician and natural philosopher Isaac Newton; and first US president George Washington.[3]

The only description of the building's interior before the first round of significant alterations comes from a report written sometime after 1944 by Mrs. Robert K. Fletcher, head cataloger, who had been in her position since 1929 and ably described the building in some detail.[4] According to Fletcher, the library included an impressive collection of paintings, hung on the walls of the lobby and the periodical and reading rooms, that included Flemish, Dutch, Spanish, and Texas artists, including two paintings by well-known Texas artist Otis Dozier that were on permanent loan, entitled "Applied Science" and "Pure Science." The paintings apparently caused some consternation between Vosper and Mr. Mayo, the person responsible for the placement of artwork within the building. While Mayo was inclined to have a neutral background for the art, Vosper was busy executing decorative treatments that Fletcher described for one of the rooms off the lobby as "walls of pink with stippled green and ceilings in green!"[5] Vosper also intended to put maps of historic cattle trails on the lower part of the walls in this room, but the concept was not implemented. Memorial plaques and portraits of important former students and college presidents were also on display; the space must have been very stimulating. However, by the time this photograph was taken, sometime between 1943 and 1946, all of the stimulation was gone and the walls had been painted a uniform color.

Another potential clash between art and decoration, or in this case art and art, was the installation of murals in the lobby sometime between 1936 and 1943. The murals were placed on the columns and pilasters, presumably to retain the walls for the hanging of paintings, and were painted by an accomplished artist named Marie B. Haines (1884–1979) with funding provided by the Federal Art Project of the Works Progress Administration. Descriptions of the murals report the topics to have been four regions in Texas: the Pine Forest, the West, the Forest Lands, and the Desert. There were also paintings in the lunettes over the doors in the room and on the wall in the grand stair. Haines also painted portraits of "Reveille," the school mascot, in 1943, which temporarily hung in the periodicals room, and "Old Gathright Hall," which hung in the music room. The painting of Reveille was lost for many years and has recently been returned to the university, but the whereabouts of the murals, which may have been painted on canvas, remain a mystery. David Chapman, chief archivist and director of Cushing Library from 1994 until his retirement in 2011, recalls that remnants of the murals existed prior to the restoration project but photographs of the murals have not materialized. (Courtesy of Cushing Memorial Library and Archives, Texas A&M University)

The lobby today is not intended to be a representation of the original design, although there are several features that are restored. Changes include the removal of the grand stair and its replacement with an elevator, the decorative painting treatment on the columns and pilasters, and the introduction of an unofficial university seal in the terrazzo floor. Restored elements include the wood wainscot and trim around doors, the basic floor plan configuration, and the column and pilaster capitals, one of the only original elements in the space.

The face on the column and pilaster capitals belongs to Sarah Orth, the daughter of Construction Superintendent William A. Orth. Since Norton's drawings do not show any faces on the capitals, this can safely be assumed to be a Vosper intervention, one that he also used on the Administration Building. The silver finish on the capitals is part of a new decorative painting scheme for the lobby that was developed by the conservator and restoration artist Johnny Langer and the design team based on an amalgam of the finishes used by Vosper in other buildings. According to Langer, there was no evidence of original decorative painting extant in the lobby. The faux-stone treatment of the columns, pilasters, and beams in the ceiling were also based on a fusion of finishes, intended as a way to creatively provide decoration to a room that was devoid of original treatments and would have therefore appeared out of place with Vosper's other buildings, and with the reading room upstairs, had a design to embellish it not been implemented.

The second floor reading room was accessed via the grand stair into the "Charging Room;" this room has been converted to an exhibit space. The primary original feature of this space is the ornamental ironwork at the entrance to the reading room, which incorporates cattle brands of the day, highlighted in gold, at left. The names of the cattle brands were documented by Head Cataloguer Fletcher and are reproduced here (*below*). (Courtesy of Cushing Memorial Library and Archives, Texas A&M University)

JO   Doc Oatman, Lockhart, Texas

SMS   S. M. Swenson and sons, Spur, Texas

U   Landergin brothers co., Amarillo, Texas

J-Λ-L   Jal Ranch, Cowden brothers, Midland, Texas

W   "Running W", King Ranch, Kingsville, Texas

LS   Clarence L. Leach, Bracketville, Texas

MK   ?

5<   Frank Wilhelm, Brady, Texas; or, "Figger Five" Clarence T. C. Davis, Maifa*;   Scharbauer, Midland

6666   S. E. Burnett Estate, Fort Worth, Texas

A   "Running A", Lee Roy McGravey, Plains, Texas

V   "Flying U", J. T. Tagsdale, Midland; or "Flying V", Matador Land and cattle co., vega

ꙅ   "Lazy S", T. W. Smith, Panhandle, Texas

Ⱶ   "E Cross", Bob Douglas, Silverton, Texas

x   Cross; W. H. Montgomery, Comanche, Texas

ᵈᵃ   "Three D's", W. T. Waggoner Estate, Fort Worth, Texas

X   "Long X", Reynolds cattle co., Fort Worth, Texas

The reading room is the most elaborate and largest room in the building, with a soaring seventeen-foot-high ceiling and three walls of tall windows. The room spans the entire width of the building's façade. The original floor consisted of a checkerboard pattern of resilient tile, most likely green and black. Wood book shelving and tall windows covered the walls. The ceiling was the star of the show, with stenciled beams and flat areas using a variety of patterns and colors. According to Fletcher, the design of the interior treatment, including the furniture, is Vosper's. (Courtesy of Cushing Memorial Library and Archives, Texas A&M University)

In contrast to the lobby where artistic license was employed in the creation of new finishes, the intention for the reading room was restoration. Prior to the removal of just about everything in the space, including the flooring, bookcases, and wall and ceiling decorative painting treatments, the original finishes were studied in preparation for restoration. Jhonny Langer, who led the restoration of the ceiling, remembers the original as poorly painted. University Archivist Chapman's research revealed that students originally painted the ceiling, a practice that was not unusual during this time. The restoration team discovered several mistakes by the novice painters including a stenciled star that was painted upside down and one long section of stenciling that was reversed. In the restoration work, the team chose to reproduce these unusual mistakes but executed them professionally, rather than poorly. Interestingly, several architecture students were recruited to work on the ceiling during the eight-month restoration process.[6] The remainder of the room was generally recreated to match the original, down to the reproduction of Vosper's furniture. A TAMU logo, in lieu of the A&M College of Texas, was added on the chairs in an effort to distinguish them from the originals.

The most elaborate decorative treatments in Vosper's buildings are usually found at the ceiling, and the reading room is no exception. The ceiling was described by Fletcher as having been executed by a young Italian decorator from San Antonio, and designed by Vosper using the "southwest for inspiration: colors of the sunset and of the desert, the flowers conventionalized native plants, the thunder bird of the Indian and other Indian motifys [*sic*] recurring in regular patterns, the Texas star and shield symbolic of the government."[7] This decorator may have been required to use students as labor to complete the ceiling, a practice that was common on the campus at the time, but that resulted in a poorly executed design. Whether because of the use of students in the execution or Vosper's focus on the other buildings that were in the design phase at the time, this ceiling remains an anomaly with respect to Vosper's other work on campus.

6

Hart Hall and Walton Hall

DATE COMPLETED: Hart: 1930; Walton: 1931

COST: Hart: $210,951.67; Walton: $243,380.03

ARCHITECT: F. E. Giesecke (S. C. P. Vosper, designer)

CONTRACTOR: Hart: William A. Orth, construction superintendent, A&M College of Texas;
Walton: William A. Orth, construction superintendent, A&M College of Texas

*"We now have Ethernet. Yes, Hart Hall in [sic] now the most
technologically advanced non-air hall on campus."*[1]

—Residents of Hart Hall, 2000

IN ADDITION to the seven academic buildings, Vosper designed two dormitories—Hart and Walton Halls—and a horse barn. Each of these buildings has been considered for demolition. With the razing of Puryear and Francis Marion Law halls fairly recently, Vosper's dormitories are the last two "ramp"-style halls remaining in use as housing. And for how long can a horse barn serve as an office building?

History

Hart Hall was built on the site of one of the earliest buildings on the campus, the Old Chapel, later known as the Assembly Hall. The Old Chapel was constructed in 1889 and was located along what was then called Chapel Street, later renamed Military Walk in 1915. The Old Chapel, which served as an assembly space for the campus, was rendered obsolete by the construction of Guion Hall in 1918, making it vulnerable to demolition when the college architect began looking for sites that would be appropriate for new housing in the late 1920s. The other buildings located along Military Walk were primarily residence halls, including Ross, Foster, Milner, Goodwin, and later Legett, Mitchell, and Bizzell Halls. At the heart of the campus and along its principal north-south circulation path at that time, the location of Hart Hall on Military Walk makes perfect sense. But over time, Military Walk ceased to be the center of residential activity on campus and many of these earlier dormitories were converted to administrative or departmental offices. This has left Hart Hall isolated from other residence halls but in a very convenient location on campus.

Hart was designed to house cadets, but after the Corps Quad was constructed in 1939, it was opened to civilians. It took until 1967 for telephones to arrive in the lounges. While a significant renovation was completed in 1974 that added carpeting, replaced exterior doors, and upgraded electrical service, air-conditioning was not installed, as students opposed it out of concern that their housing cost would rise.

The *Battalion* reported often on the residents of Hart Hall, but almost always because of their good deeds. The civic-minded behavior depicted by the residents in the occasional article may have been one reason this dorm was chosen to house women in 1978, when due to a shortage of dormitory rooms for an increasing female population, twenty-eight women were housed among the population of 280 men. According to the resident hall advisor, David Muff, who with his roommate were the only men in the ramp of women, "it is almost like living by yourself." Apparently the girls were mostly freshman and too shy to talk, and the two men could not have visitors of either sex in the evenings. The "biggest excitement" of that year was killing a roach in one of the girl's rooms.[2]

A description of the dormitory prepared by residents in 2000 provides the following advice to the student considering Hart Hall:

> Rooms were furnished with a usually functioning sink, two desks, two short dressers, a set of bunk beds, radiators that "burn the hell," one closet, towel racks and blinds. Rooms vary in size but typical is 10 × 12 feet. You can build a loft, but it must pass inspection. Paint is provided if you would like to paint your room. University does supply toilet paper. Rolls of a material believed to have been obtained from a contract with Sears, pertaining to the low sales of belt sanders [are provided]. The engineers that installed the electrical outlets in Hart Hall did so using a method believed to be associated with the game hopscotch—each room only has one plug. . . . bring an adapter.[3]

Students were told to bring their own toiletries for grooming and personal hygiene. "If you have none, than [*sic*] you need not worry, you can always move to Walton."[4]

Soon after Hart Hall, Walton Hall was completed on the site of an older residence hall called Beta Hall. Walton was very similar in design to Hart and underwent similar renovations, also resisting air conditioning units to keep rental costs down. Walton was named after President (Dr.) T. O. Walton, during whose administration (1925–34) the Vosper-designed buildings were constructed. When it opened, Walton was the largest and most amenity-filled hall on campus, prompting the name "Hotel Walton." According to the campus newspaper:

> "The hotel" is certainly not a misnomer for Walton Hall. Practically fire-proof throughout, cigarette burns on the floor an impossibility, beds in which one can actually sleep even if not completely fatigued, and bathing facilities of which the best hostelries boast are among the conveniences "the hotel" offers its occupants.[5]

The early nickname "Walton Hotel" did not stick, however, and the decorum suggested by that name turned out to be out of keeping with the behavior of some of its inhabitants. *Battalion* articles with headlines such as "Rowdy reputation leads to eviction for residents of Walton Hall ramp," "Residents of Walton get eviction warning," and "Custodians find E ramp flooded in Walton Hall" contain tales of trouble. Residents of both the E and F ramps were evicted in 1987 and 1988, respectively, and the hall was banned from the Bonfire in 1999 and the

Hart Hall circa 1935, as seen from Military Walk, is above. Walton Hall's courtyard, with landscape features as they appeared in 1940, is below. (Courtesy of Cushing Memorial Library and Archives, Texas A&M University)

The sculptural figures on top of the Old Chapel represent roles for which the men of the Agricultural and Mechanical College of Texas were being trained. The figures appear to be precariously perched and subject to winds and other forces that would lead to their decay and eventual removal. By the 1910s, the sculptures were gone, replaced with a simple pediment. This kind of symbolism would not be incorporated into another building design until Vosper's arrival. (Courtesy of Cushing Memorial Library and Archives, Texas A&M University)

Commons Dining Hall in 2000 as a result of food fights, reminiscent of the popular film "Animal House." Was it the lack of air conditioning?

Description

The halls have four stories, expressed without hierarchy on the façades. A low water table meets the ground and a simple cornice serves to cap the top of the building. Materials include the same brick found on Vosper's other buildings. Embellishment in cast stone is limited to the entrances to each ramp where ornamentation incorporates flora and fauna. The style of both dormitories is PWA Moderne.

Hart and Walton Halls are both "ramp style," a type of dormitory plan where a group of four double rooms on each of four floors share a stair and entrance—such that there are sixteen rooms and thirty-two students per ramp. Each pair of rooms shares a bathroom that is composed of a shower in one room and a water closet in another, twice the bathroom facilities offered in the earlier dormitories such as Puryear and Law. Each room has its own sink, appointed with a medicine cabinet with mirror and a light, an amenity that drew attention to these halls. Not dissimilar to the arrangements students are accustomed to

today, this style of dormitory was ahead of its time in terms of the bathroom amenities it provided. The architectural configuration of the ramps, each with its own entrance, created smaller communities within the larger hall. This type of plan was used for earlier dormitories such as Legett and Milner Halls, evolving into what at the time was considered its best arrangement in Hart and Walton Halls two decades later.

The ramps in both buildings are arranged in a U shape that is most prominent at Walton. At Hart, the courtyard is less defined and the building incorporates chamfered corners, possibly a design response to the nearby Extension Service Building, now known as the Military Science or Trigon Building. At the corners of Hart, Vosper cleverly designed reception spaces with their own entrances at the ground floor that transition to a three-room and two-bath ramp above using the 45-degree angle at the corners to great effect. Walton has a similar floor plan and arrangement on its site, providing a large courtyard on the north side. In Walton Hall, the reception rooms are located at the ends, in ramps A and K.

On the interior, the same glazed hollow clay wall tile found in the academic buildings is used for reception spaces, halls, and the stairs. Terrazzo floors and plaster walls complete the interior finishes in the shared public spaces.

This ramp-style arrangement provided a highly refined, efficient arrangement that still works today. (Courtesy of Quimby McCoy Preservation Architecture, LLP)

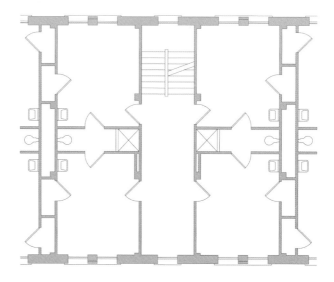

The construction of Hart and Walton Halls was a direct response to a serious housing shortage experienced for over two decades. By 1908, a group of tent structures (*top left*) was located across Main Street from the Simpson Drill Field and directly in front of the YMCA Building, which was supposed to serve as the welcoming hall for visitors to the campus. What a sight it must have been to pass by what was called "Tent City" on your way into the campus proper—not exactly the welcome anticipated by Giesecke in his 1910 campus plan. The tents were improved as wooden shacks, and an assembly hall and shower structures were constructed, prompting a name change to the "Hollywood Shacks (*middle left*)," at left below, as it appeared before 1925. So, it remained until 1928 when Puryear and Law Halls were completed, alleviating some of the housing shortage with 108 rooms each. In 1930, the *Battalion* reported that the campus held 900 rooms for rent to students with an additional 350 rooms projected as needs. The state legislature adopted a plan to increase the cost of renting in dormitories in order to raise funds for the construction of new housing. The college increased rent by $40 annually in 1930 and another $20 in 1931. With the completion of Hart Hall, there were still 153 shacks remaining in Hollywood. The cost increase was to remain in effect until all of the shacks could be demolished, which was finally accomplished soon after Walton Hall was completed in 1931 with another 176 rooms. In July 1931, rent on campus was reduced from 10% to 9% of valuation per year. (Courtesy of Cushing Memorial Library and Archives, Texas A&M University [*left*] and Courtesy of Sam Houston Sanders Corps of Cadets Center, Texas A&M University [*below*])

A big step up from Tent City and the Hollywood Shacks, Hart and Walton Halls were state of the art in the 1930s but have since become two of the least modernized residence halls on campus, both having fought the introduction of air-conditioning for many years, and won. In 1998, the university again tried to add window units, but students were adamantly against the proposal because it would increase the cost of the rooms from $525 to $956 per semester. Window air-conditioning units would not come until the twenty-first century. Because of student intervention, these two halls remain not only among the oldest and most historic halls on campus, but also the most affordable.

Befitting its purpose as a dormitory, the building demonstrates Vosper's capacity for restraint with respect to the use of ornament, at least in this instance. The use of decorative cast stone is limited to entrances to each of the ramps, where ornament flourishes. For added importance, the entrances are incorporated into a cast stone surround that includes the first floor door and the second window. The surrounds for Hart Hall are as carefully designed and crafted as any of Vosper's cast stone embellishments, incorporating *anthemia*, acanthus leaves, flowers, and other abstracted figures and moldings.

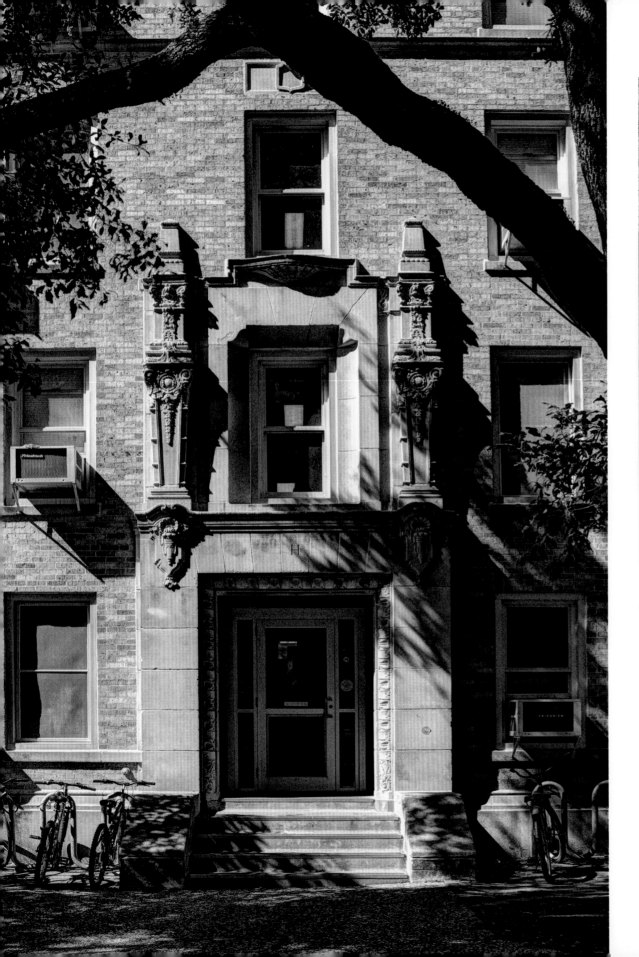

The flowers and the elegant details in the cast stone decoration at the entrances to the "Walton Hotel" belie later activity on the part of some of its residents.

Lower Jaw Of Mastodon

Mammoth Tooth In Jaw Bone

Limb Bone

Mammoth Tooth

The Petroleum Engineering, Geology, and Engineering Experiment Station Building

DATE COMPLETED: August 1933

COST: $201,714.80

ARCHITECT: F. E. Giesecke (S. C. P. Vosper, designer)

CONTRACTOR: Henger & Chambers Company

"Architectural savagery"

—Term used to describe the removal of the tower from the building
as recalled by restoration architect Harold Calhoun in 1986.[1]

ONE OF the most decorated of the Vosper buildings, with references to fossils, rocks, minerals, and trilobites, this building retains its historic character despite the removal of the tower that made this the tallest building on campus at the time of its construction. Like the Chemistry and Agricultural Engineering Buildings, the preservation of this building has benefited from what has essentially been the original user and the attention of a long-time building proctor.

History

This building was designed to house the Petroleum Engineering and Geology Departments, along with the Engineering Experiment Station, which was headed by college architect F. E. Giesecke. The contract for construction of this building allowed only 150 days for completion. The contract was signed with the same contractor, and at the same time as that for the Veterinary Hospital nearby, which had to be completed in only 110 days. Prior to letting the contract, the board of directors omitted two elevators from the construction contract but added window screens that were apparently left off the drawings by accident.

When the Petroleum Engineering Department moved into the W. T. Doherty Petroleum Engineering Building in 1961, the College of Geosciences took its place, and the name was changed to the Geology and Geosciences Building. The first significant alteration to the building was a dramatic one: the building's colorful tile tower was removed in 1972 due to suggested structural problems. In 1977, the name changed again to the Michel T. Halbouty Geosciences Building. Michel T. Halbouty '30 was an internationally renowned geologist and an independent oil and gas operator and producer in the United States. He is quoted in an article about the renaming of the building as saying, "It is the most beautiful building on campus and I am proud. The building was named after me, and it is going to be there forever."[2]

A substantial addition at the rear of the building with 59,572 square feet of space was completed in 1984. Architect Golemon & Rolfe Associates Inc. of Houston designed the addition to barely touch the original building and to blend with the adjacent 1930s structures. The first significant renovation was contemplated while the 1984 addition was under construction. As told by Christopher Mathewson, building proctor at the time, on November 25, 1984, the Building Committee of the Board of Regents recommended the denial of construction funding for this renovation because "Geology has just received a new building." A member of the architectural team in attendance alerted Mathewson to the Committee's recommendation, propelling Mathewson to take Polaroid photographs of the poor condition of the building, including water damage, rusted windows, and other health, welfare, and safety issues. Mathewson brought the photographs mounted on cardboard to the board of regents meeting the following day. When the board vote to eliminate the funding came up, Mathewson was given the opportunity to speak. Instead, he delivered the photographs as evidence of the need for a renovation. After passing the images around, the Chairman asked, "How can anyone work in this environment?" Mathewson replied, "Sir, you have a dedicated faculty

This 1959 photograph shows the tower and the colorful tile and cast stone pattern of its roof, a feature meant to be seen from a great distance. Reportedly, the tile and cast stone panels that clad the tower were salvaged after they were removed one by one and can still be found in the backyard patios of faculty members around College Station. (Courtesy of Cushing Memorial Library and Archives, Texas A&M University)

and staff!" The renovation project was immediately approved by unanimous vote.[3]

The renovation project was completed in 1986 at a cost of $3.6 million. Mathewson described the project in an article in the *Battalion*: "The only parts of the building that will be left untouched are the main lobby, which has been recognized by the Texas Historical Commission for its unique tile design, some stained glass windows and an auditorium on the first and second floor."[4] The architect for the renovation was CTJ+D of Houston, a firm that specialized in historic preservation, and the contractor was Starstone Construction of Houston.

Description

This four-story building has a ground floor with three floors above that and a basement space below the lecture room. The building is designed with the *piano-nobile*, a full flight of steps above ground, providing at-grade access to the lowest level. The ground floor acts as a base for the first and second floors, and the third floor, which is separated by a cast stone belt course, serves as a traditional attic story.

There are three entrance vestibules on the main façade, but the center entrance is clearly the most important, located under the tower that made this building an instant landmark on campus. Mexican tile panels flanking the central entrance describe the building's use with "Geology" on the left and "Petroleum" on the right, since changed to "Geophysics." The lowest level and the tower are clad in cast stone, while the rest of the building is of buff brick with cast stone accents and colorful Mexican tile panels between the windows. The original steel casement windows have been replaced with aluminum. The style is PWA Moderne with more ornament than is typically characteristic of that style.

The building is T-shaped. The front wing houses the laboratories, classrooms, and offices, interspersed on all four levels. The long leg of the T, behind the front wing, houses the two-story lecture room, here called an auditorium, which connects to the lobby on the first-floor level. Behind the auditorium, at the end of the wing, is a four-story section that was dedicated to the Engineering Experiment Station. This section, segregated from the rest of the building, was served by its own elevator and stair and was only connected at the third floor, where classrooms and offices are located over the auditorium.

Each of the three front entrance vestibules, which contain full flights of stairs, are richly decorated with cast stone tracery, cast stone shell walls, and river rock murals. At the top of the stairs are the front doors, each with ornamental ironwork with geological symbolism. The entrances all lead to a central corridor that leads to a rectangular lobby at the center of the building. The lobby features a dark marble and metallic gold color scheme with terrazzo floors in two tones of green and walls that feature three kinds of marble. The ceiling, as with most of Vosper's important spaces, was the star of the show, with concrete and plaster-covered beams, decorated with colorful stencil patterns; this treatment no longer exists. Two doors from the lobby lead to the auditorium and the elevator is located in the center of the space. According to the architectural plans, the second floor had a similar lobby, but only remnants near the elevator exist today.

The auditorium is a large space with stepped seating and a curved stage area with a very long chalkboard in the center and smaller boards to the sides. The ceiling is lower at the stage, and the wall above the stage includes ornamental cast plaster lighting sconces, paneled plaster with swags that was intended to be used for portraits of leaders in the field with framed plaques with their names, and other ornament. The walls are of plaster and the leaded stained-glass windows are designed with rock forms in subtle colors. The primary feature of the room is meant to be the ceiling, which originally included acoustic tiles painted with geometric stencil patterns, geologic symbols, and borders in a variety of bold colors. The ceiling no longer exists.

The diagram at left depicts the plan arrangement of the building—the *parti*—with emphasis on the public and most important spaces of the building which lead to the auditorium. The diagram at right depicts the vertical arrangement of these same spaces starting from outside the building and into the auditorium. (Courtesy of Quimby McCoy Preservation Architecture, LLP)

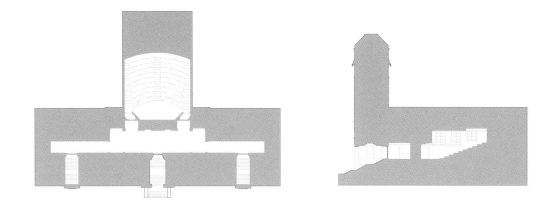

The design of the tower can be seen in Vosper's original drawings, with all of the detail considered and drawn with immaculate precision. The tower, which was 105 feet, 6 inches tall, started as a square in plan and as it rose, converted to an octagonal shape. At each of the eight corners of the octagon were concealed lights that lit the side of the tower and cast stone tracery at the openings, including one window located to enable the changing of the incandescent light bulbs, a frequent occurrence. The decorative treatments increase as the tower rises until the crescendo at the top of colorful glazed tiles in an elaborate geometric pattern. Ironically, the tower had a very mundane purpose—it housed a large tank holding hot water. The reason for the tank installed at that elevation was to equalize pressure in the hot water lines of the campus steam heating system. A new power plant made this system obsolete in 1964, making it possible to remove the tower and tank eight years later. (Copyright 2016 Texas A&M University)

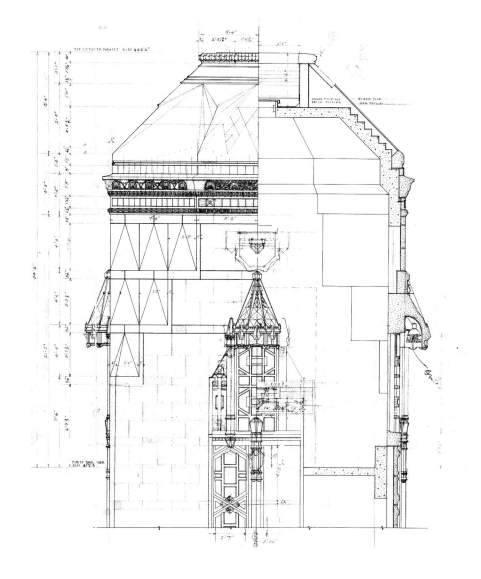

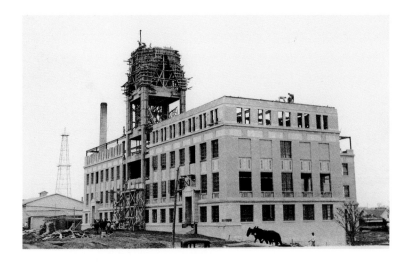

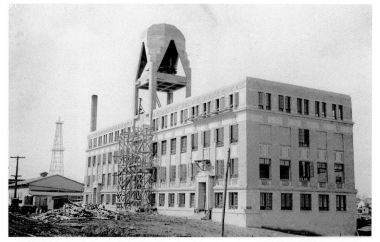

The tower removal "savagery" remains a conflicted story: was it necessary, and was there no reasonable way to repair the tower? Like many buildings on the campus, this one was supported by expansive clay soil, and cracks, though not extensive, had not gone unnoticed. However, it was the "rattling" of the tower during high winds that apparently had the university most concerned. Eventually the tower was deemed a "safety hazard and too expensive to repair." "Cast stone facings in the tower are loose and there is a danger they could fall. The tower will be down in a month," reported Paul W. Stephens of the TAMU System on August 3, 1972, presumably with the intention of completing the removal before the return of the full student body for the fall semester.[5]

Consistent with the adage "what goes up, must come down," the construction process described in these historic images shows how a steel frame was encased in concrete to create a concrete dome beneath which the water tank could sit. The concrete dome was then covered with cast stone panels and finally decorated with glazed tile in various colors. As described by Mathewson, the deconstruction of the tower involved a similar process starting in reverse with the removal of the colorful clay tiles piece by piece. The cast stone was then removed, after which the concrete dome could be separated from the rest of the building. The steel frame connecting the shell to the rest of the building would be cut at the last minute. A crane was brought in and set up to lift the tower, as soon as the last piece of steel was cut. However, the massive concrete structure was far heavier than had been

anticipated, and the crane was not sufficiently counterbalanced. Once the crane made connection with the tower and began to engage it to lift, the unbalanced weight caused the crane to tilt forward. Thanks to the swift response of a bulldozer operator who was there to load the debris from the demolition on the ground, disaster was averted. The bulldozer operator put his loader bucket on the tail of the crane and pulled it back to an upright position. A larger crane was then called in to complete the job. (Courtesy Cushing Memorial Library and Archives, Texas A&M University)

The color that was lost with the removal of the tower remains in the Mexican tile panels between windows, also called spandrel panels. It is easy to imagine how having this bold and lively color at the very top of the tower's roof would have been the perfect complement to the repetitive pattern, color, and the occasional trilobite on the façades. However, not everyone was a fan of the color and decoration on this building. Ernest Langford, head of the architecture program in the College of Engineering at the time Vosper taught, wrote the following in 1963 when the tenets of modernism were firmly established in the pedagogy of the college's architecture program:

> Architecturally, this building beggars all description. It is in the shape of a capital T in plan, four stories in height, and possesses a veritable wilderness of cast stone features, spandrel after spandrel, of multi-colored tile work, and a tower out of all proportion to the purpose for which it serves. . . . The roof of the tower is finished in ceramic tiles of vivid colors and intricate patterns—all of which is lost because of the height.[6]

One wonders if a similar comment would be made about the ornate geometric design of the top of the Chrysler Building when it was completed in 1930. A small section of the demolished tower is on display on the east side and behind the building.

The Mexican tile floor at the landings of the vestibule stairs feature one of the most vivid and colorful of the floor tiles Vosper consistently included at the entrances to these academic buildings. The tile here is most vivid because it has been well protected from sunlight. The tile is set into a green terrazzo stair landing. According to project manager for the TAMU System, W. Howard Bagett, who in 1972 was involved in the removal of the tower project: "The tile, figure heads and mosaic are a reflection of Mexican architecture. . . . Vosper was in love with a girl in Mexico, and it influenced his work."[7]

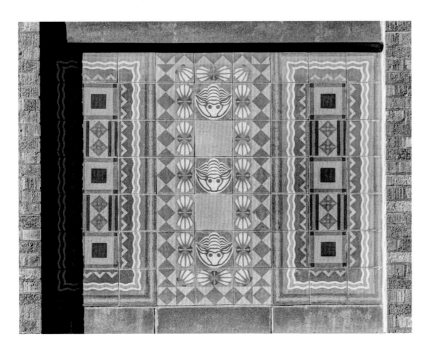

The design of the entrance vestibules does not hold back on decoration. Not only is the floor green with inset brilliantly colored tile, the walls are also embellished with heavily textured stone panels created from shells. On the original architectural drawings, these shell panels are shown to be of petrified wood, but apparently, there was a substitution. The ceilings are decorated with a variety of strange symbols that include stars, a crescent moon-face, cherubs performing various activities, and abstract forms. Metallic paints are used in conjunction with a bold yellow and blue color for these ceilings, which means every surface is covered in decoration: ceiling, walls, and floor, each distinct yet somehow harmonious with one another.

The cast stone ornament in all three of the vestibules is impressive, yet different from that on some of the other buildings by Vosper. For example, the tracery at the flanking entrances is often found in ecclesiastical architecture (*above*), while the river rock mosaic of a flower pot is more pedestrian (*right*).

The ornamental ironwork on the entrance doors incorporates traditional geometric forms combined with stylized references to geology. In 1999, James L. Keith of Galveston recalled his experience working with the college architect while he was an architectural student in the summer of 1931. He was given the task of designing and detailing full size the wrought iron gates for the Petroleum Engineering and Geology Building and was to depict trilobites in the design, of which he writes: "Vosper guided me and so did Phil Norton, who did most of the nuts and bolts work at the College Architect's office. I wonder if the gates are still in place in the building's foyer. And if so, if any students know what the design depicts?"[8] These ornamental iron and glass doors are still in use, whereas they have been replaced on other buildings. It is presumed that the reason they remain here is that there is an accessible entrance closer to grade level where a lighter door is available.

Lobby

The lobby was designed to function, on both the first and second floors, as an "Exhibit Foyer" where the departments housed in the building could display collections of rocks, minerals, and other educational material. The floor is made of two tons of green terrazzo, the walls are plaster with a marble wainscot, and the ceiling is plaster and was originally stenciled with a border on the flat areas and geometric patterns on the concrete beams. The plaster ceiling and the cove lighting that are there today are not original. The marble wainscoting is composed of three marbles: starting from the bottom of the wall at the base are breccia sanguine red (of stalagmitic origin from Algeria), a band of green Tinos (an ophicalcite stone from Greece), and above that an unidentified black marble with extensive gold veining (*below*). As with other buildings designed by Vosper, a display component always celebrates the building's function. The lobby thus functions as an exhibit hall, a gathering place, and a reception lobby. Later, the lobby came to be named the Hall of Honor, recognizing individuals who have endowed three chairs in geosciences, four professorships, and seven fellowships and scholarships. Houston artist David Adickes, best known for his sixty-seven-foot-tall sculpture of Sam Houston in Huntsville, Texas, created a life-size bronze of Halbouty, unveiled in April 1988. The statue depicts Halbouty leaning on a lectern, his arms cradling a geophysical log from his first well, which is currently displayed at the center of the first floor lobby (*right*).

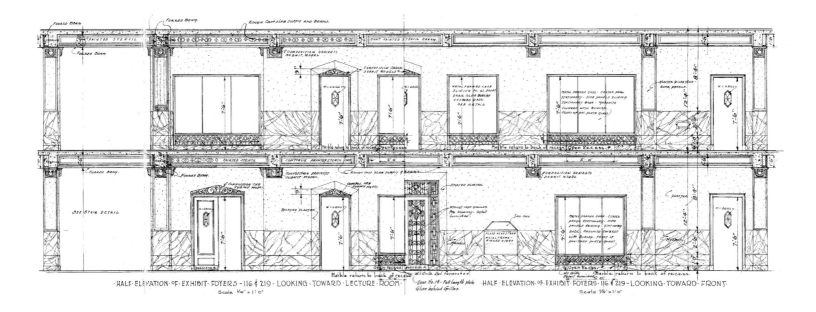

·HALF·ELEVATION·OF·EXHIBIT·FOYERS·116 & 219·LOOKING·TOWARD·LECTURE·ROOM·
Scale ¼" = 1'0"

·HALF·ELEVATION·OF·EXHIBIT·FOYERS·116 & 219·LOOKING·TOWARD·FRONT·
Scale ¼" = 1'0"

A remnant of the lobby that was designed for the second floor remains at the elevator, with the same plaster door surround and marble wainscot as is found in the first floor lobby. The original drawings indicate that the lobbies on the first and second floors were both display spaces, an arrangement also found originally in the Agricultural Engineering Building. The extensive stencil decoration that was part of the ceiling design can be seen here. It is not known if this design was ever executed, and no evidence remains of this treatment to confirm its existence. While other academic buildings by Vosper have very elaborate decorative lobby ceilings, only this and the Veterinary Hospital lobbies featured stenciling on the beams as shown here, and neither of these two buildings retains evidence of its original treatments. (Copyright 2016 Texas A&M University)

The capitals of the plaster pilasters that appear to support the concrete beams of the ceiling feature charming castings of a trilobite nestled amongst greenery. A study of the historic finishes revealed that this element was originally finished in a dark, bronze-colored paint that matched the pilasters, display cabinets, and other trim in the lobby. What is seen today represents several paint layers over the original.

The auditorium retains many original features that will continue to be preserved in an upcoming renovation led by the university's Classroom Improvement Committee. The renovation includes new flooring on the concrete stepped floor, repairs to plaster walls, audio-visual and lighting improvements, and restoration of the historic painted finishes scheme. Matthew J. Mosca, historic paint finishes consultant, prepared an historic painted finishes investigation. This investigation found that plaster walls were painted in a pale tan-pink color not unlike the terrazzo floor in the room, and doors, trim, and grilles were painted with special finishes that include the same umber glazing and ragged or stippled technique found in the Agricultural Engineering Building. Stained glass windows, the stage platform, ornamental metal grilles, and black slate chalkboards will be retained. The ceiling has been removed and replaced, most likely with the removal of asbestos; no record of the tiles remains. Ernest Langford described this ceiling as having "a multiplicity of stenciled patterns in a variety of colors,"[9] making it the most colorful on campus, and the original architectural drawings support this description. However, without evidence to support its original appearance, it cannot be reproduced.

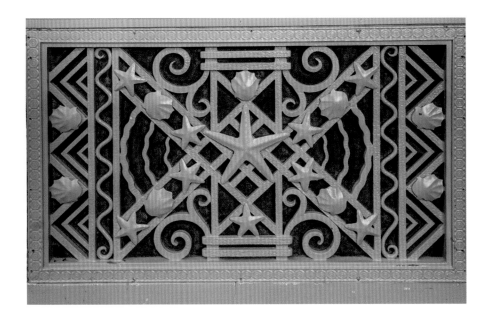

Custom grills like this one were created for each of the Vosper buildings, here with a pattern composed of geometric shapes, seashells, and the symbol of the Lone Star State. The original finish on this grill is a faux dark bronze created with a base of aluminum paint covered with umber glaze applied unevenly with a ragged or stippled technique.

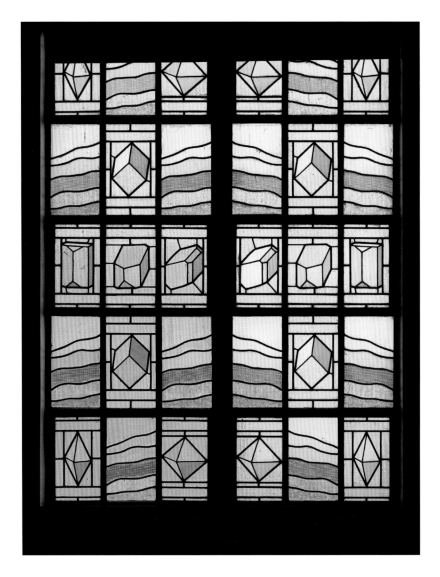

The leaded stained glass windows, which pick up the gold, blues, and greens that are found elsewhere in the building, depict stylized geologic crystal formations. The crystal forms depicted include the cube, octahedron, and prism, and between the crystals are suggestions of geologic layers.

Stairs

While not as important as the auditorium with its stained glass and special finishes, this stair is typical for the stairs in all the Vosper buildings, which are both for daily use and for emergency egress. A window at the landing, since covered here, provided natural light; the floors are of green terrazzo; the walls are of glazed hollow clay tile in a mottled tan color that is also used throughout the corridors as a wainscot; and the ceilings are flat plaster. The warmth of the glazed tile walls, which in certain light looks golden, combined with the rich green terrazzo and the simplicity of the design, makes the stairs as pleasing as any other part of the building.

Special light fixtures adorn each of Vosper's buildings, some repetitive and some that are one of a kind. This faceted style of globe mounted onto a plaster ornamental medallion is typical of the way these fixtures were designed but is suggestive of crystal forms that are particularly appropriate for this building.

8

The Veterinary Hospital

DATE COMPLETED: August 1933

COST: $142,852.48

ARCHITECT: F. E. Giesecke (S. C. P. Vosper, designer)

CONTRACTOR: Henger & Chambers Company

"Old Aggies who knew the Civil Engineering Building when it was the Veterinary Hospital had one special request when the building was vacated for remodeling: save the exterior stonework."[1]

—*The Battalion*, 1984

THE VETERINARY Hospital building displays some of the best cast stone work on campus, and beyond, a fact that was not lost on the former students who insisted the stonework be preserved. While the exterior ornament with its unique assortment of animal heads has been retained, the interior was completely gutted in the second round of renovation undertaken to better serve the Civil Engineering Department that has occupied the building for the last sixty years. This is the only one of Vosper's buildings to have completely lost its magnificent interior spaces.

History

The School of Veterinary Medicine, as it was called at the time, had a propitious beginning, has outgrown its physical facilities many times, and continues to do so today. The school started as a result of the Texas cattle fever, also known as Texas fever, which threatened the state's cattle industry in the late nineteenth century. The threat to cattle nationwide was attributed to the Texas longhorn, which carried a disease transmitted along cattle trails that was nearly always fatal. The closing of Kansas-to-Texas cattle entirely, together with restrictive legislation passed by many other states, was an important factor in ending the Texas cattle-trailing industry. In 1893, Theobald Smith and Fred Lucius Kilborne of the federal Bureau of Animal Industry in Washington, DC, announced their isolation of the pathogen of Texas fever. They demonstrated that the disease is caused by a microscopic protozoan that inhabits and destroys red blood cells.[2]

Dr. H. J. Detmers, a pathologist from Germany, was sent to Texas by the US Secretary of Agriculture to study this disease. This study led to A&M's decision to start a new program in veterinary medicine, to be led by Dr. Detmers. But Detmers had made a commitment to Ohio State University and could not accept the offer, so he recommended Dr. Mark Francis. Dr. Francis, who later became one of the foremost veterinarians in the country, was thus given the opportunity to lead the new veterinary medicine program. Before the Texas cattle fever was eradicated in this country, nonimmune American cattle were protected from it by elaborate federal quarantine laws separating southern cattle from others in railway cars and stockyards. Northern cattle imported to the south for breeding purposes could be immunized by receiving injections of small amounts of blood from infected animals. Francis was a pioneer in the development of this method of immunization. His fight against the fever tick and his work in developing a method of immunizing cattle gave him an international reputation and the cognomen "Father of the Texas Cattle Industry."

Francis became a professor of veterinary science at A&M in 1888 and taught classes in Old Main. In 1902, a large structure was erected in the general location of what is now Cushing Library, primarily to serve chemistry, but also housing veterinary science. It was known as the "ChemVet" building. The establishment of a School of Veterinary Medicine to be led by Francis in 1916 created the opportunity for a new purpose-designed building, named Francis Hall, completed in 1918. The school very quickly outgrew that facility, however, and sought a larger building by 1930 with more laboratory and hospital space where students could put science into practice. In Francis' own words:

It was the latter part of July or the first of August when I arrived at College Station. The college work at first was merely some classroom lectures to the agricultural students. There were no laboratories or equipment for this work. We had a room about 14 × 16 feet that was on the ground floor of the Main Building (destroyed by fire in May 1912) that served as office, classroom and laboratory. At the end of the school year (June 1889) the adjoining room became vacant and was assigned to us as a classroom. In this unsuitable place we toiled for 15 years. There was no hospital. Along about December 1888, a frame barn was built to serve this purpose. It was about 20 × 36 feet and was near where the Agriculture Building now stands. The following year a frame building was provided that served as a dissecting room.

Eventually, in the 1930s, the veterinary hospital building was erected along with an anatomy building and stables to provide the students with useful hands-on learning opportunities. The veterinary hospital has been one of the cornerstones of CVM's history and academic prowess. As a teaching hospital, it still provides students with real-life medical cases while also providing much needed services to the community.[3]

Thus the name of the Vosper-designed building was the Veterinary Hospital, and the most important space in that building was the clinic space—the equivalent of the elaborate lecture rooms that were the principal spaces in the other academic buildings. The construction contract was let with the Petroleum Engineering Building to a single contactor who had only 110 days to build this structure and the accompanying barn. However, this building too was obsolete just twenty years later and, in 1954, a "new" veterinary medicine building was completed on what is today called the West Campus, a location that provided ample room for future growth. That building was expanded several times leading to another new building for the Veterinary and Biomedical Education Complex in 2016.

As soon as veterinary medicine moved to the West Campus, plans were announced in 1956 for the renovation of four veter-

The Veterinary Hospital as it appeared in 1934, just after its completion with Ross Street in the foreground. (Courtesy of Cushing Memorial Library and Archives, Texas A&M University)

inary buildings for use by civil engineering, which had by then outgrown Nagle Hall, its location since 1909. Modifications to the building were modest as both the building and the barns behind it were renovated to enable them to function as laboratories and classrooms by Texas A&M University System Architect Philip G. Norton, the same architect who had been a key contributor to Vosper's work twenty years prior. A more significant renovation came in 1984 that included the removal of everything from the interior with two exceptions: the stepped seating of the original amphitheater and the vestibule at the entrance. The building continues to function for the undergraduate program of civil engineering and as part of what is now an expanding College of Engineering complex. The building has been known as the Civil Engineering Building much longer than it was known as the Veterinary Hospital.

Description

This is the smallest of Vosper's buildings at only two stories, although each floor includes over 19,000 square feet of space. This building appears to be more formal than the others because cast stone is almost the exclusive material of the front façade, a choice Vosper otherwise only made at the Administration Building. The use of Mexican tile is also more restrained here. The rear and side façades incorporate brick as the primary material with cast stone and Mexican tile as accents. The ornament also appears to be more traditional and Neoclassical from a distance, but a closer read reveals instead an homage to animals of all kinds, including pigs, horses, cattle, dogs, sheep, goats, and chickens. There may be no better example of *architecture parlante*, or "architecture that speaks," than this building.

The façades exhibit the traditional organization with a base that is a water table of coursed cast stone instead of a basement or lower floor level. A low wall enclosing a small terrace in front of the entrance reinforces the sense of a base. The main body of the building consists of two floors that are expressed together by the use of pilasters for vertical emphasis with Mexican tile spandrels under the windows. The attic story is really a parapet wall that extends above the cornice and is itself ornamented with shallow pediments to give the appearance of more height. The steel casement windows have been replaced with aluminum. The materials include cast stone, buff brick, and colorful Mexican tile. The style is best described as PWA Moderne, although the extent of ornament on the front façade is more exuberant here than is typical for this style.

The building is arranged in an E shape. The east and west legs or wings of the E are two stories in height while the middle wing is just one story. The east wing is longer than the other two wings. The west wing housed an amphitheater; the middle wing was the clinic and as its placement suggests, the most important space in the building; and the east wing contained corridors off which were classrooms and laboratory spaces.

A single central entrance includes a slightly elevated terrace partially enclosed by a low curved wall. Off the terrace is the entrance, which leads to a small vestibule and beyond that, the lobby. While only the vestibule space remains today, the original design is understood from the architectural drawings. The entrance and lobby featured cast stone walls, a material no other

Vosper lobby had. The floors were of Mexican tile set within a marble border, and the ceiling and beams were both of stenciled concrete and plaster, like those of the Petroleum Engineering Building. To the left of the entrance was a reception room and office with an adjacent library, possibly for the department head, that included a private restroom. On the right is another office, also with a private restroom. Directly in front of the entrance is the access to the clinic space, and flanking that are two sets of stairs that lead to the second floor. The second floor corridors featured the same glazed tile wainscoting and plaster walls, terrazzo flooring, and suspended plaster ceiling that are found in other Vosper buildings.

The character of the interior of the clinic was utilitarian, and many historic images exist not of the space itself, but of the activities within, which are not always pleasant to see. While not expressed with the highly crafted materials and decoration found in the lecture rooms of other buildings, the significance of the clinic is made evident by the additional Mexican tile and brick details that are found on the exterior.

The diagram at left depicts the plan arrangement of the building—the *parti*—with emphasis on the public and most important spaces of the building that lead to the clinic. The diagram at right depicts the vertical arrangement of these same spaces starting from outside the building and into the clinic. (Courtesy of Quimby McCoy Preservation Architecture, LLP)

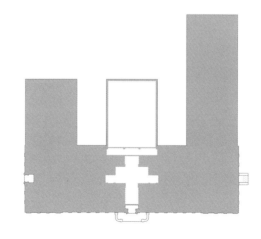

The cast stone on this building, as is the case for all of the Vosper buildings, is excellent—some of the best examples of cast stone anywhere. Cast stone as a material has traditionally been considered a second choice and more economical option when compared to natural stone carved by the hand of a talented sculptor. However, cast stone became a very popular alternative to cut stone in the 1920s, proving it to be practical because repetitive ornaments could be produced efficiently and quickly. Cast stone has been the material of choice for most of the older buildings on the campus and is still in use today. Some examples include Legett and Milner Halls (1911), the Academic Building (1914), and the YMCA Building (1914). In the hands of the designers, sculptors, and the fabricators involved in the Depression-era building program, cast stone has proven to be the best choice of material. The quality of the material composition is evident by its longevity of service and condition, which is generally excellent, with the exception of specific areas of deterioration where water tends to collect. The craftsmanship of production is also excellent, especially toward the latter part of the building program. The sculpted models, from which molds were made, are attributed to a stone sculptor of note, Hugo Villa. Villa would have used Vosper's designs, delineated on the architectural plans in detail and in some cases with full-size drawings, to create the models. However, there were most likely also times when Vosper did not draw the detail, leaving some interpretation to Villa. The two men worked well together, based on their prior and future collaborations. Records are not complete enough to know how many sculptors may have worked on this building program but one other sculptor, also an Italian named Gino Bernasconi, is known to have worked on the models for the Veterinary Hospital because of correspondence with College Architect Giesecke requesting assistance in obtaining payment from the Dallas Architectural Decorating Company, and from his involvement with the doors of the Agricultural Engineering Building. According to the architectural drawings, the cast stone would be cast at the College Stone Plant on campus set up by Construction Superintendent Orth at the start of this building program, but records also show that the Dallas Architectural Decorating Company produced cast stone for this building at a total cost of $18,000, a substantial component of the construction cost.

One of the most elaborate cast stone elements on the campus is found in the cornice decoration that forms a pediment over the central entrance and over each of the end bays of the main façade. This building, like Animal Industries, presented the perfect opportunity for Vosper to play with animal heads and skulls. While many animals get their due, the cow is prominently featured at the center, perhaps because Dr. Mark Francis's career was so significantly associated with this animal (*left*). Like musical notes, animal heads, medical symbolism, leaves, scrolls, and other ornament are composed into a harmonious whole. Beneath the cornice is a frieze that runs the length of the façade featuring cattle skulls linked by garlands made of leaves and flowers with a rosette above (*below*). This playful arrangement of ornament is an exceptional example of *agrafes*, the connection of one architectural detail to another in classical architecture.

In this detail of the shield above the main entrance, the playful character and deft sculpting of the cast stone ornament by Hugo Villa is front and center.

Hugo Villa

Hugo Villa (1885–1948) is the sculptor known to have been responsible for the creation of the models that were used to create molds for the casting of stone for Vosper's designs. Villa was born in Italy, where he studied medicine and music and later sculpture at the *Academia Albertina delle Belle Arti* (an academy of fine arts) for one year. In 1918 Villa immigrated to the United States. According to Villa, he met Gutzon Borglum, a sculptor of international acclaim best known for Mount Rushmore, in New York in 1919 and was associated with him for about 20 years.[4] Borglum moved to Texas in 1925 and Villa either came with him, or soon joined him, settling in San Antonio. The two men were working on the Mount Rushmore project, which began in 1927 and ended with Borglum's death in 1941. But reportedly after a decade of working together, Borglum discharged Villa from the Mount Rushmore project for a mistake. The two men resumed their association not long after that however. Meanwhile, Vosper collaborated with Borglum during this period, when the two men created a plan for the bay front of Corpus Christi, unveiled in late 1927. In 1928, it was Villa and Vosper who collaborated and won a national competition for a memorial named "Texas Memorial to Honored Dead," a bronze relief that would be installed at the north end of the Memorial Stadium at the University of Texas. Vosper then brought Villa to College Station to work on his ten buildings. In a letter to David Chapman, then chief archivist for the Cushing Memorial Library from one of Vosper's former students, James L. Keith, Jr. '31 of Galveston, Keith wrote:

> I remember distinctly that all the decorative cast stone work was done on campus. The sculptor was a person brought in by Vosper who had been working for Borglum on the Mt. Rushmore Presidential facades, I don't remember his name. But I remember how amazingly deft he was with a ball of clay; leaves or spirals or architectural symbols would come to life flowing from his hands. Vosper had him come to our class room and demonstrate for the students. You can see his work now in the cast stone work of all of the Vosper designed work of that period.[5]

By 1935, Villa and Vosper were working together in Goliad where they collaborated on the Mission Nuestra Senora del Espiritu Santo de Zuniga and on the Goliad Memorial Auditorium. Villa continued to work out of his studio in San Antonio, took a break during World War II to assist with the war effort, and then started working again but died soon after in 1948. Vosper served as a pallbearer at Villa's funeral.[6] Villa's work, which includes bronze castings, plaster, cast stone, and cast concrete works, as well as carved stone, is concentrated in and around San Antonio, including Goliad, Refugio, New Braunfels, Brazoria, Austin, and College Station.

Vosper's collection of photographs includes several images of Villa's models like this one, taken in 1932. In this example, the model is for a cast stone panel and consists of six flags representing those that flew over Texas surrounding a shield representing the A&M College of Texas. This panel can be found on the east (front) façade of the Administration Building at the end walls of the loggia. These same representations for the six flags can be found on the interior within the hanging light trough that is the centerpiece of the Great Hall. (Courtesy of Cushing Memorial Library and Archives, Texas A&M University)

This is a plaster model of Dr. Mark Francis. Villa created a bust of Francis that was donated to the college by Professor D. W. Williams in June 1933. It is not known if the bust was displayed in the new Veterinary Hospital but if it was, the bust left the building with the school. His present location is not known. (Courtesy of Cushing Memorial Library and Archives, Texas A&M University)

Villa was also responsible for the flagpole monument that sits in front of the Administration Building. Donated in part by the Class of 1934 (which donated $800; another $2,000 came from the landscape architect, F. W. Hensel), the monument was installed in 1934 with the completion of the landscape at the new east entrance to the campus. The monument is best known for its "Littlest Cadet" relief, shown here. The flagpole monument was replaced in 2014 with a replica of the original.

preservation practitioners have nearly abolished this practice due to the irreparable damage it causes to the stone by removing the outer surface and patina, thereby opening up the material to taking in more water and soiling, leading eventually to more degradation.

In this detail of the cornice at the main entrance one finds a cornucopia—a symbol used often by Vosper and one befitting Vosper's design approach. The cornucopia is a symbol of plenty, consisting of a goat's horn overflowing with flowers, fruit, and corn, or anything suggesting abundance, as in an abundance of cast stone ornament.

Dr. Donald McDonald was the department head for Civil Engineering during the $2.5 million "gut" renovation that was undertaken to return the building to academic use from administrative offices that had been the primary objective of the earlier renovation. According to McDonald, this renovation sought to provide more classroom space, laboratories, and project rooms and was the first work undertaken at the building since Civil Engineering moved into it in 1956. It was determined, as it often is for the sake of expediency, that removing everything from the inside would be ideal. It is not clear if there was an intent to modernize the exterior of the building also, but former students made sure the cast stone was saved. In the words of Dr. Robert M. Olson, who served as the liaison between the department and the architect and builders, "Old Aggies who knew the Civil Engineering Building when it was the Veterinary Hospital had one special request when the building was vacated for remodeling: save the exterior stonework." Thus, "stonework will be retained at the request of former students . . . but will be carefully cleaned and sandblasted," Olson said.[7] Ironically, what Olson clearly did not know is that sandblasting the cast stone actually damages the material. While more common in the 1980s, today's historic

Although the overall impression of this building is of a light gray-colored cast stone, color and pattern were not left off the building completely. This colorful Mexican tile and pig head spandrel panel that sit between windows provide just the right amount of respite from the gray and buff tones of the masonry. More patterns and colors are found on the end and rear façades, where the primary material is brick and the relief is cast stone and Mexican tile.

Historic photographs of the interior of the lobby of this building have not been found, so it is not known precisely what the lobby looked like. It is assumed that there were similarities between this and the Petroleum Engineering Building next door, based on the architectural plans that show similar ceiling treatments featuring decorative stencil patterns. Differences included cast stone wainscoting here instead of marble and Mexican tile floors instead of terrazzo, but both had painted plaster walls and concrete and plaster ceiling beams with stenciled decoration. We do know from Vosper's other buildings that the interior would have been special and is irreplaceable—not the sort of interiors that are typically found in institutional settings since. These interiors could have happened only when they did, when the Great Depression made manual labor and craftsmanship more affordable, when ornament was still in use, when materials tended to be hand produced rather than machine made, and last, but not least, when Vosper was around to make the most of these circumstances.

Today, there is far more awareness of the value of these interiors, and it is unlikely that another interior like this one will be gutted. In the meantime, we are left with a single reminder of what the building's interior once was: the bold pattern of color in the Mexican tile floor of the vestibule.

9

The Administration Building

DATE COMPLETED: October 1933

COST: $362,774.34

ACHITECT: F. E. Giesecke (S. C. P. Vosper, designer)

CONTRACTOR: Standard Construction Company

"The administration building is an outstanding example of Mr. Vosper's ability. One can hardly believe that a designer who could do, say, the building for animal industries could reverse himself and do a building so thoroughly classic as this. All tile work is gone, exterior decorative ornament is reduced materially—what is used appears largely in the cornices and in details around doors and windows. But having divested the exterior of the building of all extraneous tile patterns and most of the animal heads and figures, Mr. Vosper pulled out all the stops in his treatment of interior walls, the main stairway, pilasters, ceilings and floors. . . . All things considered, the administration building is by far the most grandiosely conceived structure ever erected on the campus of Texas A&M College." [1]

—Ernest Langford, 1963

THE ADMINISTRATION Building, now known as the Jack K. Williams Building, was designed by S. C. P. Vosper to be the frontispiece of the new plan to reorient the campus toward the east. Vosper's passion for the state's history, landscape, and culture radiates from every detail in the building. If architecture speaks, Vosper used this design to welcome visitors to the campus, to celebrate the agricultural and mechanical roots of the institution, and to present some of the state's history, while providing offices to serve the president and other administrators. The building may have also communicated a need for preservation because this is appropriately one of the least changed of Vosper's buildings.

History

From the very beginning, it was clear that this building would be as important to the campus as the Academic Building, which faced the west entrance. When the construction bids came in higher than expected, the board approved them anyway with instructions to look at cost savings that would not affect the usefulness or appearance of the building. It was designed to house the president's office, the registrar's office, and the fiscal office, as well as offices of the dean of the college and deans of the various schools. The Texas Forest Service occupied the entire third floor, and the Agricultural and Mechanical (A&M) Press and publicity offices were located on the ground floor.[2] The building would serve as the frontispiece of the reoriented campus and its new east entrance facing Highway 6, responding to the change from trains to cars as the predominant mode of transportation. Once the building was completed in late 1933, construction of the entrance approach and landscape followed.

The Standard Construction Company (changed to Fretz Construction in 1934) built the Administration Building. Construction is rarely easy or without potential conflicts, but apparently the company performed well. In a letter on other topics from the construction administrator for the college, A. B. Granger, to project manager G. W. Gartner of the Standard Construction Company, dated October 16, 1933, soon after the completion of construction, Granger wrote:

We wish to assure you at this time that we have thoroughly enjoyed our relation with the Standard Construction Company and all members of your staff and sincerely wish that it were possible for you to secure further work from the College. We should like you to know that we appreciated your efforts to cooperate with us in all matters and the cheerful way in which you complied with some of the red tape here at College, which we know must have been tiresome for you.[3]

Small alteration projects began as early as 1942 with a reshuffling of occupants. In 1948, the Texas A&M System was created to manage the evolution of a statewide education, research, and service system. When the Coke Building was completed in 1951, the president's office was moved there, and the Administration Building became known as the System Administration Building, and home of the chancellor of the Texas A&M University System. The first significant alteration came in 1952 with this change of use and the introduction of the Agriculture Extension Service and the Agricultural Experiment Station to the building. Designed by college architect Arch C. Baker, modifications were designed to match the existing architectural vocabulary. When additional office space was needed on the first floor, Baker spared no expense when he moved the ornate iron and stained-glass partitions and doors that separate the Great Hall from the registrar and fiscal offices, thus preserving this significant feature. Air-conditioning and other changes occurred through the 1950s and 1960s and were generally respectful of the original design. It was not until the 1970s that changes became more obvious, with dropped ceilings installed in an effort to conserve energy and the use of less-expensive materials for interior alteration work.

In 1986, Harold Calhoun of CTJ + D of Houston, an architect with a specialization in historic preservation, led the exterior restoration of the building that included the refinishing of the ornamental front doors, cleaning and repair of the cast stone, and the replacement of windows, using the campus standard aluminum window customized somewhat to simulate the originals. This exterior restoration project cost $868,000. Other

Vosper-designed buildings received a face-lift around the same time, at the ripe old age of 50 years, including the Petroleum Engineering Building and the Veterinary Hospital. In 1997, the building took on another new name, this time to honor Dr. Jack K. Williams, the seventeenth president of A&M and the Texas A&M System from 1970–79 and chancellor of the System from 1977–79. Williams was president during one of the university's greatest growth periods. Enrollment went from 10,000 to 20,000 students during his presidency.[4]

The entire first floor remained empty after the College of Agriculture moved out around 2010 and until the 2014 completion of a capital renewal project meant to replace aged air-conditioning, plumbing, and electrical systems and introduce a fire-suppression system and other life safety and accessibility improvements. Concurrent with this project was the relocation of the president's office from Rudder Tower, where it had been located since 1989. Other than the systems replacement work, no changes of note were made to accommodate the president and his staff within the original president's suite on the second floor. Likewise, no funding was in place to restore any of the special materials, ornamental ironwork, and decorative treatments in the public spaces or on the exterior. Designed by Quimby McCoy Preservation Architecture of Dallas and constructed by Vaughn Construction of College Station, the project cost $9.5 million and left as much of the historic fabric as possible undisturbed while integrating new systems and improvements.

President R. Bowen Loftin '71 may have had some help making the decision to move out of Rudder Tower, which was slated for renovation work of its own. As the story was told to the author by a retired administrator, the decision to move the office was made not long after a visit from then president and chancellor of Baylor University, Kenneth Starr. Apparently Starr drove from Waco to College Station and upon pulling into the entrance to campus on New Main Drive noticed the monumental building directly in front of him and immediately concluded that this must be the home of the president's office. Starr parked and walked into the first floor to find it completely empty. The only directory was left behind years ago by the College of Agricul-

ture. Somewhat bewildered by the underutilized but beautiful interior, he called the president's office to find out exactly where the office was located. Once Starr made his way across campus to Rudder Tower, he mentioned this experience to Loftin, emphasizing the inherent contradiction in message that the Administration Building conveys to the visitor. A few years later,

Fritz W. Hensel '07 was the landscape designer responsible for the east entrance to the campus and for helping Giesecke reorient the campus toward the new State Highway 6. Hensel, a native of San Antonio, came to the college in 1903 as a student and left only long enough to obtain his master of science degree from Cornell University in 1914. He taught in the Department of Horticulture and in 1926 became the first head of the Department of Landscape Art, a position he held until his death in 1949. Hensel designed the east entrance using principles such as axial planning, a processional sequence of spaces, and symmetry, which fit well with Vosper's building. In addition to planning the new entrance, Hensel introduced live oak trees to the college, along New Main Drive, which cost $1.95 each. Concurrent with the completion of the new east entrance, funding was made available for a beautification plan designed by Hensel that including planting trees and shrubs across the campus. This executed planting can be seen in many of the historic images from the 1930s and early 1940s and was similar in style to that seen in the photograph here. Hensel also designed Hensel Park, which was named in his memory. (Courtesy of Cushing Memorial Library and Archives, Texas A&M University)

This was the view upon arrival to the campus's New Main Drive after 1934 and the completion of Hensel's landscape design and the flagpole installation. Note the Animal Industries Building's "wedding cake" profile on the left and its sister building, Agricultural Engineering, on the right. Although hard to understand today, when Giesecke presented the new plan for a reoriented campus to A&M's board of directors on February 12, 1932, apparently the only building for which the board questioned the placement was the Administration Building. However, the location was approved at that same meeting. (Courtesy of Cushing Memorial Library and Archives, Texas A&M University)

the president's office was relocated along with those for finance, administration, the provost, and other members of the president's cabinet. By that time, Loftin had left the university, and interim president Mark A. Hussey and, later, president Michael K. Young had the opportunity to move back to the building originally designed for this purpose eighty years earlier.

Description

Four stories high, the building is a rectangle in plan and elevation. Here Vosper chose to use more Neoclassical details and forms. The monumentality expressed by the building conveys the growing importance of the A&M College of Texas.

The façades are clearly arranged using a *piano-nobile* and hierarchical arrangement. A base, which is distinguished with a darker tone of cast stone with deeper reveal joints, is also the ground floor level. The *piano-nobile* is the first floor, one full level above ground. This floor and the second floor are delineated by a two-story high colonnade of bright white Ionic columns that extends over the majority of the front façade. Tall windows denote the importance of the floors within, and the front doors are covered with ornamental iron grills. Finally, an attic story, which is the third floor, with smaller windows and an elaborate cornice treatment complete the composition. The roof is hipped and of copper with an integral gutter system. The entire building is of cast stone ashlar blocks. Cast stone urns and planters adorn the entrances.

The style is Neoclassical and Moderne, with Art Deco–style ornament, and few animal heads thrown in here and there. Decoration is rich and of the highest quality, from the ornamental bronze doors with figures depicting agriculture and mechanics set within stained glass to the lions' head gargoyles at the very top of the cornice.

The rectangular form of the plan is simply organized around a Great Hall that connects the ceremonial east entrance doors with the campus-side west entrance. The Great Hall is a two-story open space with a central grand staircase on the east side of the room and balconies on the other three sides. The walls are treated with an Italian decorative treatment called *scagliola*, which in this building mimics travertine stone. The floor is of patterned terrazzo in a variety of colors. The ceiling features what appears to be a carved wood (it is actually made of plaster) floating light trough that is richly painted in deep red, green, blue, and with plenty of gold leaf. Around the ceiling are moldings treated with gold leaf, and the ceiling itself is a deep ultra-marine blue.

Off the Great Hall are shorter halls. On the first floor, these halls, which feature ornamental iron and stained glass partitions with doors, originally led to the fiscal office on the north and the registrar's office on the south. On the second floor, this arrangement was repeated but with a narrower hall to the offices of the president and dean of the college on the north and quarters for the other deans on the south. The third floor spans the Great Hall and is organized by a central corridor leading to offices.

The diagram at right depicts the plan arrangement of the building—the *parti*—with emphasis on the public and most important spaces of the building that lead to the Great Hall. The diagram at far right depicts the vertical arrangement of these same spaces starting from outside the building and into the Great Hall. (Courtesy of Quimby McCoy Preservation Architecture, LLP)

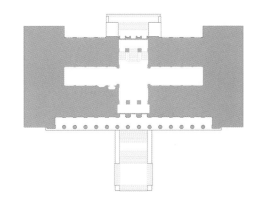 

The Administration Building is designed to be seen from a great distance; it is also designed to welcome the visitor to an established and thriving institution. Likewise, the approach to the building and the campus at large has similar aspirations. The first decision made was to place the building on axis with the campus entry to avoid any potential confusion about its relevance. The next decision was to place the building far away, in the distance, from the entrance gate along State Highway 6 and to the extent the existing terrain would allow, to raise the building to a higher plane. Both of these design decisions create a dramatic and heightened sense of arrival. The experience of entering the campus starts at the gate and New Main Drive, which is lined in live oak trees to emphasize its length and axial relationship to the building in the distance. New Main is interrupted before it reaches the building with a semicircular drive that forces the visitor to go around the building to reach it, to either the north or south. This allows for a large front lawn that adds to the sense that this is a monument of a building. At this point, the pedestrian experience starts with four slowly rising stepped walkways that were originally lined with low-lying plantings and hedges that no longer exist. These walkways were part of a *parterre* garden, a French term for a formal, ornamental garden with paths that is typically symmetrical. The Palace of Versailles has perhaps the best-known *parterre* garden in the world; by association, Hensel signified the importance of his design. The *parterre* garden ends in a terrace that features semicircular walks at each end and cast stone balustrades and low walls that define an outdoor anteroom from which the visitor can begin ascending the grand stair to the building itself. All of this planned sequential experience, also known as a procession, is part of the *Ecole des Beaux-Arts* doctrine that is the basis for both the landscape and architectural design of the campus built during the Depression era—a bit of irony in retrospect, but greatly appreciated today.

The elaboration of the entrance experience creates a monument out of the building and also signals its ceremonial function. Here, countless Corps of Cadet classes have been photographed, former students' weddings celebrated, and other special events held. The front of the building can be said to be a ceremonial entrance and is not the entrance used by most faculty, students, or visitors (above). On the west-facing, campus side of the building is a second entrance consisting of three doorways (right). While just as magnificent a design as those at the ceremonial entrance, these doors are not as tall, and instead of leading directly into the Great Hall, these doors lead to a midlevel landing or vestibule. A short flight of steps above the ground on the campus side also make these doors less important and more accessible to the everyday user. The hierarchy of the entrances is clear.

Raiford L. Stripling was the designer, under Vosper, of the campus side entrance. As recounted by Stripling, Vosper said "I'll take the front, you take the back."[5]

One of the most discussed "Vosperisms" on the building may be the use of a female face, alternating with that of a male, on the otherwise classical Ionic column capitals of the colonnade of the ceremonial façade. In 1933, only men were admitted to the A&M College of Texas. Women were permitted to take classes, and later could graduate, but only if they were the wives or children of employees of the college. Hence, it is surprising to find the female face in such a prominent location. The accepted theory, espoused by Ernest Langford, is that the face of the male was meant to represent an "idealized cadet," derived from Greek and Roman warrior sculpture, while the female was meant as a companion. This theory is logical, but so are two additional possibilities. The first is that the male and female faces represent agriculture and mechanics, a theme Vosper used unsparingly elsewhere on the building. The second theory is that Vosper intentionally included women as a statement of his own. During the design of the building, the subject of women being admitted was a controversial topic being debated by the board of directors and surely by everyone on campus at the time. It may be that Vosper was of the opinion that women either would be admitted soon, or should be. How was he to know that it would take another thirty years for women to be officially admitted in 1963?

The face of the female was modeled after Sarah Orth, who was later married to Distinguished Alumnus J. W. Aston '33 of Dallas. Her father, William A. Orth, was superintendent of construction for the college.[6] Ms. Orth became a student the year following her short modeling career. Her face was also used inside Cushing Library and on the light trough inside of this building.

Not one to leave an animal out, Vosper reserved for the very top of the most important building on campus the lion's head, which can be found along the cornice interspersed with the classical *anthemia* ornament (*left*). Oddly, the corners are treated with a cherub. A smaller lion's head is used on each side of the planters on the loggia, much closer to the visitor; these have been described by some as "peeking out from behind" the planters, an example of Vosper's wit at play (*below*).

The theme of Texas's history, a topic that Vosper reveled in, sometimes literally, is seen as soon as the visitor ascends the grand stair and through the colonnade into the loggia space that provides cover for the entrance doors. Above each of the twelve windows and three sets of doors is a cast stone panel depicting part of the state's history. Above the center door is a representation of the first public institution of higher education, with Mother Nature in the center presiding over male figures representing animal husbandry (*left*) and agriculture (*right*). The tools held by each figure address the "mechanics" component of the college. Above the doors to the left and right are the inscriptions "Austin" for Stephen F. Austin, the father of Texas, and "Lamar" for Mirabeau B. Lamar, the father of education in the state. The panels above windows provide another reference to the Lone Star State, featuring the head of a Longhorn. At each end of the loggia is another panel depicting the six flags that flew over Texas surrounding a shield meant to represent the college. The references to Texas start here but are continued throughout the building.

Note the play on scale with the exaggerated *anthemion*, or honeysuckle, ornament used here at Stripling's entrance, which is combined with a pineapple to symbolize "welcome." The American eagle in the background is a formal reference that would be used only on a very important building, above. On the right is an urn at the campus-side entrance. Despite a coating treatment that obscures some of the detail, the urn displays the quality of the cast stone material and its durability as well as the talent of the artists and craftsmen. A reptile that appears to be climbing onto the urn contradicts the classical fluted Ionic column.

These bronze doors at the campus-side entrance use male and female figures to represent agriculture and mechanics, one of Vosper's favorite themes. One of the earliest depictions of figures to represent the purpose of the college was a sculptural element located at the top of the 1889 Old Chapel Building, later known as the Assembly Hall at the present site of Hart Hall. This sculpture can be seen in the earliest photographs of the building but was removed in the 1910s. The sculpture included three male figures representing agriculture and mechanics: On the left is an engineer with a saw, in the center is a man about to hammer a block, and on the right is a farmer with a plow. This detailed depiction of the men and their activities would have been an iconic element for the early college (page 5 and page 91). Figures representing this theme were not used again until Vosper. At the Administration Building alone, this theme is expressed on the flagpole monument in front of the building, possibly on the column capitals, in the bronze doors of both the ceremonial and campus entrance, in the light trough of the Great Hall, and in the lounging figures above doorways off of that space. The theme applied to the bronze doors of the campus entrance is particularly appealing with its Art Deco style decoration in relief on the metal, at left, and equally delightful when seen from the inside, lighted with sunlight, with the colorful stained glass background, at right.

This historic image demonstrates the variety of patination originally present in the bronze doors. Today, the patination has aged to a uniform brown color; the artistic treatment and distinction between the elements is lost. In order to retain the distinction, the bronze would need to be waxed or sealed as part of its regular maintenance. Without this protection, the bronze will oxidize and revert to its natural patina over time, which is a dark brownish-gray color with some green. (Courtesy of Cushing Memorial Library and Archives, Texas A&M University)

The ironwork on this building was produced by Voss Metal Works of San Antonio and includes the ornamental bronze ceremonial and campus-side entrance doors, window grilles, interior ornamental iron and glass partitions, ornamental ventilation grilles, and custom hardware. This lunette, of which there are three located above the three campus-side doors, still displays some of the variation in the bronze patina that would have been seen originally. There would have been at least two, and possibly three, levels of patina on the bronze in order to distinguish certain features. For example, the sun rays might have been a bright golden bronze color with no patina, while the bronze behind them may have had a darker patina. For more information on Voss Metal Works, refer to the Agricultural Engineering Building, (pages 156 and 157).

Vosper's appetite for ornament and his desire to enable the building to speak for itself led to his creation of a number of shields and cartouches to represent the subject matter associated with each building he designed. For the Administration Building, he took this idea one step further and created a logo for the college. The logo can be found in the front doors of the ceremonial entrance and is often missed by visitors because of its subtlety. It features the letter A and the letter M superimposed upon one another. The college never adopted the logo, but it remains a unique and artistic example of the agriculture and mechanics theme. Voss Metal Works of San Antonio cast the bronze doors; to this day, the company displays the logo in its conference room in two tons of bronze that enable the letters to be read clearly.

The room also features soft pinkish-tan colored *scagliola*, an Italian treatment for plaster on the walls. *Scagliola*, pronounced without a hard "g" as *scagl-io-la*, is an Italian term for a method of treating plaster to imitate various types of stone, which here is travertine, a type of marble. The process involves the use of pigments and other additives within the plaster that are then mixed or swirled and cast into a mold, and then polished, to create a panel or other forms. The technique can be traced back to the Roman architect Vitruvius and is often used as a way of imitating precious or expensive stones. Although it simulates a natural material, the substitute in this case is an artistic endeavor and may be equally or more valuable than a natural material for that reason. Melba Marini Champion, daughter of Carlos Marini, recounted her father's work on the building in a letter following a visit to the campus. Carlos Marini emigrated from Italy and established the Houston Art Stone and Staff Company, which was hired by the contractor to decorate the interior of the building. Champion recalls how "ugly the building was until after the 100 stone masons, mostly Italian, worked for one year to make it beautiful." Champion calls the decoration "imitation Travertini," which translates to travertine in English.[7] Her letter has caused some confusion due to her use of the words *stone* and *masons*, suggesting that this decorating company had worked on the building exterior, but that was not the case. The beauty of the interior *scagliola* is only visible in some areas off the

Great Hall that are now part of offices. The remainder of the *scagliola* is still there but it has been painted over and glazed in an unsuccessful effort to simulate the original. In this photograph (*right*), taken during construction in 2013 after a mail chute was temporarily removed thereby exposing the original surface, the painted simulated treatment can be seen next to the real thing. Someday, the "scag" walls of the Great Hall could be restored. (Courtesy of Quimby McCoy Preservation Architecture, LLP)

The Great Hall (*above*) is a ceremonial room in which one can spend hours discovering the unique details, decoration, and artwork that have been carefully integrated into its design. It is also a well-proportioned, two-story space, with light coming in from the tall west-facing windows and from windows on the balcony level. Originally designed to have stained and leaded glass that was never installed, these tall west-facing windows brought in too much sunlight and heat. In the 1960s, the original glass was replaced with purple glass. This decision caused the room to appear too dark and purple. In the 2014 renovation, the purple glass was removed and replaced with clear glass in order to bring more light back into the space. A slight tint was used in the glass to reduce the light levels and to better blend with the existing window glass, and a small amount of the purple glass was left in place around the perimeter of the windows. A grand staircase leads to the balcony at the second floor and the office of the president (above). Architecture students have been required to sketch this space for many years, as a part of their studies.

This hall and another one opposite of it are open to the Great Hall, and the partition at the end is the ornamental iron and glass partition that was moved approximately thirty feet in 1952. The partition is made of steel that has been hammered to give it texture and painted with a faux-bronze finish. Here reside three doors featuring leaded and stained glass in vivid colors. Note the vaulted ceiling in this space, which retains the original glazed and stippled painted treatment that can also be seen in the Agricultural Engineering and Animal Industries Buildings. The rich, almost leather-like appearance of this painted treatment, where it is still visible, is in good condition.

The colorful stained glass takes on the theme of Texas with familiar symbols are shown here. These three panels are found in the doors of the ornamental iron and glass partition. The cowboy is found on the partition doors on the south side of the Hall (*left*), the star is found on the center doors and on wood doors leading from the Great Hall (*center*), and the stagecoach is found on the partition doors on the north side (*right*). The architectural drawings refer to the stained glass as "Belgium Glass." The Pittsburgh Plate Glass company supplied it, but the designs are certainly custom made.

One of the most magnificent features in the Great Hall is the floating light trough, set off by the deep blue ceiling around it. The light trough provides indirect light in the form of a cove and direct light from a central fixture. The cast plaster trough is also highly ornamental and richly decorated. One male and one female bust on opposite ends of the trough are surrounded by a combination of chevron decoration and Roman (or Greek) figures, all bordered by a variety of geometric and classical moldings in gold leaf, accented with deep red, blue, and green colors. The green is seen again in the ceiling of the adjacent balcony on the second floor. Here the male torso with its tools is meant to represent the mechanical side and the female torso surrounded by wheat, the agricultural side of the college. In the center of the trough is a star surrounded by the six flags that flew over Texas; this element is also a light source. Raiford L. Stripling designed the trough, under Vosper's direction.

Within the space, the trough is not easily admired in detail because much of it is seen in silhouette and the light levels in the room are low. The photograph here provides a unique opportunity to see exactly how the trough is decorated.

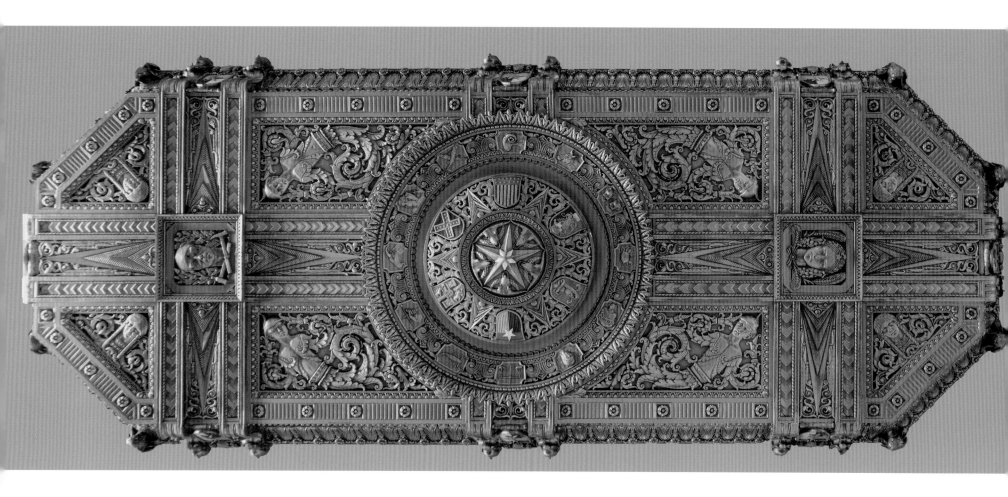

Not to be outdone by the ceiling, the floor includes a twelve-foot diameter circle in which a map of Texas, oriented to true north, is depicted entirely in terrazzo. The map showcases natural and historic sites in Texas, including rivers, trails, missions, battle sites, and most important, the location of the state's oldest public institution of higher learning. The following places are depicted on the map, which is re-oriented here to enable easier reading:

Aluminum strips: major rivers of Texas

Patches of color: ecological regions of Texas

Brass strips: historic roadways and cattle trails (Cattle trails are also represented with a brass circle with inlayed steer head.)

Maroon circles with brass inlay of crossed sabers: Texas battle sites

Brass circles with cream-colored infill: early settlements (Spanish and Anglo colonization)

Large cream-colored star with brass inlayed domed building: capitol of Texas (Henry C. Dethloff has pointed out that the state capitol is indicated on the wrong side of the Colorado River.)

Large cream-colored star with brass A&M inlayed: the Agricultural and Mechanical College of Texas

Brass circles with inlayed stars: earlier capitols of Texas (Washington-on-the-Brazos and Houston)

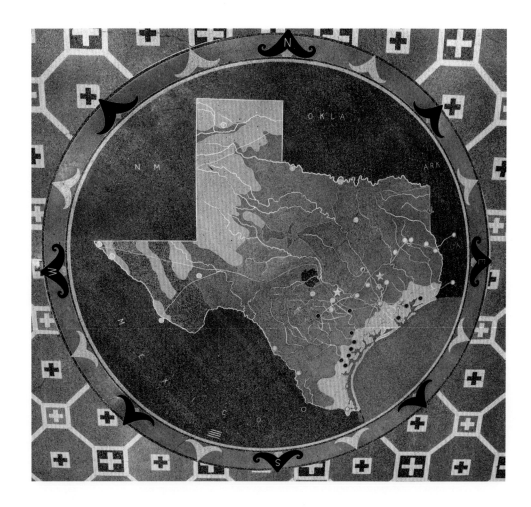

The office of the president moved out of the Administration Building in 1951 when the Coke Building opened. From there, the office moved to Rudder Tower in 1989 and then back to the Administration Building in 2014. Here is the president's office as it appeared in 2015, essentially unchanged from its 1933 appearance. The office has windows on the north and east sides and three doors lead into the room. The fireplace is the focal point. For many years, a portrait of President T. O. Walton hung over the fireplace. Walton served as president during the Depression-era building program that left the college with Vosper's architectural legacy.

THE HARDY PLOWMAN'S TOOLS
THE NEXT MUST KNOW
WHICH WANTING, WE CAN
NEITHER PLOW NOR SOW
VERGIL.

TO TEA
THE STREAM A BETTER COUR
AND TILL THE WILD.
AND DRAIN THE FEN. AND
STRETCH THE LONG CANAL
DY

10

The Agricultural Engineering Building

DATE COMPLETED: October 1933

COST: $191,245.85

ARCHITECT: F. E. Giesecke (S. C. P. Vosper, designer)

CONTRACTOR: Walsh, Burney and Key, Inc.

"Part of the extraordinary attention given to the appearance of these buildings were the painted finishes that were employed. That architect S. C. P. Vosper worked on theaters prior to working on the buildings at Texas A&M is not a surprise because the painted surfaces within these buildings show a knowledge of the tradition of specialty painting that was associated with theaters of the early twentieth century." [1]

—Matthew Mosca, 2016

THE AGRICULTURAL Engineering Building is one of only three academic buildings designed by Vosper that is still serving its original users. There is a sustained connection between the Department of Agricultural Engineering (now the Biological and Agricultural Engineering Department, or BAEN) and its building that began with Dr. Daniels Scoates, department head from 1919–39, for whom the building was renamed in 1945, and continues with the current department head, Dr. Stephen Searcy, who now advocates for the building. For most people on the campus, however, the building is known for its front door—made of remarkably delicate, intricate, and beautiful ironwork.

History

The Department of Agricultural Engineering sought to replace its wooden farm-type buildings beginning in 1923, at which time they were described as inadequate compared to facilities at peer institutions like the University of Minnesota and the University of Nebraska.[2] Thus, when the building program started in the late 1920s, the Department of Agricultural Engineering had already established its need for a new facility, putting them in a good position to obtain one. Located on the Agricultural Quad, a feature of the newly reoriented campus, the new building was reportedly developed with Daniels Scoates' (1882–1939) intimate involvement. This is substantiated by Scoates' personal plea to the board of directors to keep a lifting crane that was part of the building's design when cuts were being discussed after the construction bids came in higher than expected. During a special session of the board to review the bids for construction of the building and to discuss a policy for construction in general on the campus, the board determined that the crane was not necessary and voted that it be removed from the plans and the space be utilized for other purposes. Ultimately, not only did the crane get taken away, but the building was also reduced in size by two window bays, or approximately 15 percent of the rear wing. Furthermore, the board suggested to Mr. Walsh, the contractor, that he use student labor, to which Walsh responded that he would be glad to use as many students as he could.[3] Scoates was also involved in defining the requirements for the

building. The era of automotive farm equipment began around the time Scoates came to head the Department in 1919, and the display and study of this equipment was at the cutting edge of technology in its day. In addition to the mechanization of farming, rural electrification and housing for farmers were of keen interest to Scoates and, hence, to the Department. The building is designed specifically for the use and maintenance of motorized farm equipment with a novel rotating and elevating display platform within the lecture room stage that allowed students to see the equipment from all vantage points. Scoates also reportedly expressed a preference for an "Agricultural Engineers Hall of Fame" to commemorate leaders in the field, which was provided in the lobby. Only six years after his death, the building was renamed Scoates Hall in his honor.

Scoates Hall was designated a "Historic Landmark of Agricultural Engineering" by the American Society of Agricultural Engineers in 1978 because of its unique design and ornamen-

This image was taken just after construction was complete in 1933; the Agricultural Engineering and the Animal Industries Buildings face one another across what was at the time called the "Agricultural Quad," a term that never stuck. The two buildings share many similarities, one of which is the elaborate ironwork at the entrances, and they share a *parti* that involves three parts: the front wing for academic purposes, the middle for the lecture room, and the back wing for practical applications spaces. (Courtesy of Department of Biological and Agricultural Engineering, College of Agriculture and Life Sciences, Texas A&M University)

tation and because of its association with an agricultural engineering leader, Daniels Scoates.[4] Scoates had been a member of the American Society of Agricultural Engineers and a former president, and he maintained a strong connection between the college and that professional organization. Perhaps this early recognition of the building's historic significance played a part in the strong stewardship and association that the Department maintains with the building today.

In 1959, significant renovations to classrooms and public restrooms were designed by System architect Henry D. Mayfield, Jr., followed by central air-conditioning, suspended ceilings, and a new exit stair addition designed by Harper, Kemp, Clutts and Parker Architects of Dallas in 1968. In 2014, the building underwent a significant renovation that replaced all of the mechanical, electrical, and plumbing systems; added a fire suppression system; and addressed life safety and accessibility needs. Quimby McCoy Preservation Architecture, LLP of Dallas served as architect for the project and Vaughn Construction of College Station as the construction manager. The project cost $9.6 million. As a result of Department Head Searcy's tenacious efforts and willingness to raise, beg, or borrow additional funding, and with the help of the Classroom Improvement Committee and the Office of the Provost, the lecture room was restored as part of this project, and later the exterior was repaired, just in time for the centennial celebration of the agricultural engineering program in 2015.

Description

Three stories tall, with the lower level partially below ground, the building presents a simplified version of the traditional organization for the façades. A cast stone water table forms the base; the first and second floors together form the body of the building, united by their spandrel panels; and the third floor acts as an attic story in that it is separated by a heavy belt course from the rest of the building. The *piano-nobile* is on the second floor.

The front door, memorable for its elaborate ornamental ironwork, is located at the midlevel between the first and second floors. A front stoop consisting of a few steps and two landings of colorful Mexican tile lead to the entrance. At the top landing

The Avery Tractor Company tractor in the foreground dates to 1918 and was displayed at the college at Agricultural Engineering Fairs through the 1930s, as shown in this photograph of the west side of the Agricultural Engineering Building taken sometime after 1933. The tractor's journey included many years on the campus after it became an orphan when the company declared bankruptcy in 1924 and finally dissolved during World War II. At that point, *de facto* property of A&M, the tractor was most likely stored in the building for many years. The Institute of Texan Cultures borrowed the tractor from A&M for the World's Fair in San Antonio, HemisFair '68, where it was displayed and then remained on exhibit indoors for at least forty more years. The Institute then moved it outdoors until around 2011, when the Institute decided it was time to return the tractor to A&M. But there was no place at A&M to store the tractor, so Department Head Searcy found it a new home with the Buice family, which maintains a collection of historic tractors, with the stipulation that the tractor be brought back to A&M for display at the department's centennial anniversary celebration. The Buice family restored the tractor and returned it as promised, where it was displayed once again in 2015.[5] Perhaps the tractor will be on display yet again as part of the Buice's collection of 1911–28 tractors near Waco.[6] (Courtesy of Department of Biological and Agricultural Engineering, College of Agriculture and Life Sciences, Texas A&M University)

are found two poems. On the left-hand side is a poem from the *Georgics*, Greek for "On working the earth," a series of books by the Roman poet Plubius Vergilius Maro, more commonly known as "Vergil" or "Virgil." It reads: "The hardy plowman's tools / we next must know, / which wanting, we can / neither plow nor sow." On the right side are lines taken, imprecisely, from the poem *The Fleece* by Welshman John Dyer that reads: "to teach / the stream a better course, / and till the wild, / and drain the fen, / and stretch the long canal."

The façade materials include cast stone and buff brick with colorful Mexican tile panels as the spandrel panels under the windows. The original steel casement windows have been replaced with aluminum. A projecting cast stone cornice with a fascia of colorful tile and perched owls tops the building. The style of the building is PWA Moderne.

The form of the building is divided into three parts—these parts correspond to the plan *parti*. In the shape of an asymmetrical H are three distinct forms that correspond to academic knowledge in the front wing and practical application in the rear wing, with a lecture room in the middle where these two purposes come together, figuratively and literally. The front wing serves as the main entrance leading to a vestibule. Polished black marble walls, colorful green and blue Mexican tile floors, and an elaborately painted ceiling greet the visitor. A stair leads to the lobby, or "Exhibit Foyer," a rectangular room that is also treated with black marble walls, terrazzo floors, and a highly ornate ornamental plaster ceiling with an agricultural theme. Indirect lighting hidden in troughs that are integrated into the ceiling design provide uniform lighting. At each end of the space are dramatic portals flanked by four niches, each designed to hold a bust of a person associated with the manufacture of farm equipment. On the floor above are faculty offices, and on the floor below are graduate student offices and laboratories,

originally for such topics as rural electrification and irrigation and drainage. The lower level originally included a large exhibit space, directly below the main floor's "Exhibit Foyer."

The middle wing contains the most important space in the building, the lecture room, which is entered from the lobby. The lecture room is a two-story high space with stepped seating and a stage with a platform large enough to accommodate a tractor. The ceiling is the main architectural feature of the room, painted in a silver color with stenciled patterns in green and blue. A vividly colorful mural with six sides is located above the stage. In the middle of the H form of the building, the academic discipline of the front wing and the practical hands-on use of the rear wing come together at the stage. Here a large opening connects with the rear wing, enabling tractors and other farm equipment to be driven directly onto the stage, where a hydraulic lift and rotating round platform could be used to fully display equipment to the audience. This novel feature is reminiscent of the movable floor that Vosper designed for the Scottish Rite Cathedral in San Antonio.[7]

The ground floor of the rear wing provides large and flexible space with higher ceilings than the other floors of this wing and slab on grade construction to support the heavy farming equipment that was housed there. Above this at-grade level are two floors of classrooms and laboratories that originally included a "Farm Building Laboratory" occupying the entire rear wing area on the third floor.

For anyone who knows this building, it would be impossible not to mention the confusion this three-part plan *parti* causes a new or even novice visitor. The only floor that connects to all three parts of the building is the third floor. Luckily, there are multiple entrances on the outside of the building (a total of six) that are generally used instead of traveling to the third floor to make connections.

The diagram at right depicts the plan arrangement of the three parts of the building—the *parti*—with emphasis on the public and most important spaces of the building that lead to the lecture room. The diagram at right depicts the vertical arrangement of these same spaces starting from outside the building and into the lecture room. (Courtesy of Quimby McCoy Preservation Architecture, LLP)

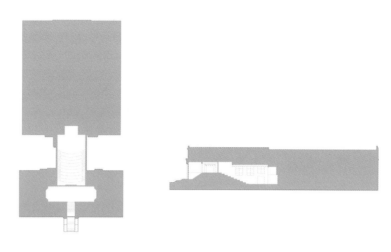

The cast stone on this building, as with the other buildings, demonstrates Vosper's use of *architecture parlante*, translated as "architecture that speaks," as well as his wit. A combination of agricultural crops and the friends and foe of agriculture surround the entrance (*left*). Rats climb next to ears of corn and grain sorghum. Nearby, oversized boll weevils, an agricultural pest, and bees, the source of pollination, coexist among plant materials, outlined in cotton bolls and leaves (*right*).

Vosper's choice of a rat could not have foretold the 1983 infestation led by "Kit Kat Mouse," so named for the animal's preference for a brand of candy. As described by the *Battalion*, 140 rats were killed within a six-week period after getting into the candy in vending machines as well as fish food, plants, sugar, rice, glue, laboratory supplies, and over fifty pounds of dog food.

The *cartouche*, or shield, over the entrance serves as an artistic representation for the department and features a sun, river, grain, and sickle—all components necessary for agriculture. Beside the shield are four Latin words: on the left are *potentia* and *aqua* (power and water), and on the right are *machinae* and *edeficia* (machinery and buildings). Flanking the shield is a pair of *cornucopia*, or goat's horns, brimming with nature's bounty. Surrounding the shield, out of view in this image, are four smaller shields representing farm equipment, including the hoe (soil cultivation), the plow (soil preparation), the flail (crop processing), and the sickle (harvesting).

The prominent ironwork at the entrance features an elaborate and delicate combination of traditional forms and stylized agricultural subject matter. Close inspection reveals a mix of wheat plant parts including leaves, florets, grain heads, and possibly seeds, pods, leaves, flowers, and acorns (left) surrounding a back-lit A and E superimposed on one another for "Agricultural Engineering." The A and E logo, set against the blue background color, was also back-lit for maximum effect (right). But, that was still not enough for Vosper. From scant available evidence left beneath screws and on the sides of ornament, an investigation of the painted finishes determined that these doors were originally a blue-gray color, similar to the blue color in the Mexican tile, with highlights in gold leaf, green, and red—a bold design. While it no longer stands out with these bold colors that coordinated with the patterned tile on the façade nearby, this is still one of the most beautiful entrances on campus.

The original pair of doors that were part of the ironwork is no longer on the building. The doors were removed, the surrounding ironwork was sandblasted, repainted, (leaving very little evidence of the original paint), and discarded. Rescued by a family member of former Department Head Price Hobgood, the original doors are still in use today on a barn at a ranch near Hico, Texas. The replacement doors for the building are similar but lack the intricate detail and charm of the original, which featured two birds facing one another, shown here. The birds were originally highlighted with gold leaf and the flowers were red. (Courtesy of Quimby McCoy Preservation Architecture, LLP)

Voss Metal Works

Theodore (Theo) Voss, of Voss Metal Works in San Antonio, is the man responsible for the ironwork on this and other buildings of the same period, including the Administration Building and the weathervanes at the Horse Barn. Theo Voss was the son of a German immigrant *Bacher der feinen Waren*, or baker of fine goods, an artistic profession, who arrived in the United States via Galveston to Santa Monica, California, where Theo was born in 1901. When his father died two years later, Theo moved to Wittenburge, Germany, with his mother, where he was raised, learned the trade of ironworking through the guild system, married, and had son, Kurt Voss. Theo then moved to San Antonio where he set up Theodore Voss Artistic Scroll Metal Work, a company that went out of business during the Depression. Theo then set up a new company called Voss Metal Works. His son Kurt was taught the trade and continued the business after his father's death. Kurt Voss changed the company name to Kurt Voss Metal Works and in turn taught the business to his son Ted Voss, who now operates the company as Ted Voss Metals Inc.[8]

Theo Voss worked closely with Samuel Vosper at A&M College, in San Antonio, and in Goliad. Theo Voss, Raiford Stripling, and Vosper were good friends, according to Theo's son Kurt Voss. Kurt remembers Vosper as a friendly, talkative architect who was easy to get along with but who did not own a car and therefore had to be driven everywhere. Hugo Villa was also a friend of the group and often worked directly with Voss Metal Works.

This photograph is of Theo Voss and his son Kurt on the steps of the nearly completed Agricultural Engineering Building's impressive ironwork entrance. The company also produced the lighting in the building, including the two exterior stanchions, the pendant lamp in the vestibule, and the wagon wheel and farm implement "chandelier" in the lecture room. Eighty-five years later, Kurt and Ted Voss provided information, including the photographs included here, that aided the restoration of the lecture room chandelier and the documentation of the colors on the original entrance doors. Geno Bernasconi, who worked under Hugo Villa, is credited as the model maker for the doors, which Villa pronounced "beautiful." (Courtesy of Kurt Voss and Ted Voss Metals Inc.)

In this photograph, the grill for the entrance to the building is in the Voss Metal Works factory located in downtown, San Antonio, now a residence. The company has relocated to the northern side of the city. (Courtesy of Kurt Voss and Ted Voss Metals Inc.)

Voss Metal Works also produced the bronze doors on the east and west entrances of the Administration Building and ornamental ironwork for other buildings of the Vosper era on campus. Note that the date on the photograph of the Administration Building doors is September 1934, one year after the building was considered complete by the college architect. The discrepancy of the date has to do with a claim made by a hardware provider seeking payment and the photograph was most likely taken to prove to the college that the doors were in fact fabricated and ready for delivery, pending the arrival of the hardware. (Courtesy of Kurt Voss and Ted Voss Metals Inc.)

Color is an important element in the design of all of Vosper's buildings, with the exception of the more formal Cushing Library and the Administration Building, where the use of color is subtle. In addition to the geometric-patterned colored tile with agricultural symbols between windows on the façades of the front wing (*above*) is a band of tile interspersed with perched owls that appear to support the projecting cornice above them (*right*). The owl as the primary animal in the building's decoration is appropriate both as a friend of agriculture and as a symbol of wisdom.

Color continues to be integrated into the design on the interior in spaces like the vestibule, where the pendant light fixture and decorative paints on the ceiling share the same colors as the ironwork on the exterior. Here the ironwork of the front door is seen in silhouette against the bright sky and as a reflection on the polished black marble walls.

The lobby, referred to as the "Exhibit Foyer" on the drawings, is a long rectangular space off which are doors leading to various offices, a library, conference room, and the lecture room (*above*). At each end of the lobby are dramatic portals that were once painted entirely in silver (using aluminum flake paint) that frame a bold blue-green colored anteroom that leads to offices. The two portals incorporate four niches for the busts of men important to agricultural equipment manufacturing, but only one bust remains today. As remembered by Department Head Searcy, there were three busts remaining in the 1980s. Two of these busts disappeared until there was only one left. The remaining bust is of cast bronze by American sculptor Lorado Taft (1880–1936) (*right*). Taft was an *Ecole des Beaux-Arts*-educated artist based in Chicago who around the time of this commission created the sculpture for the Louisiana State Capital in Baton Rouge. Searcy determined that the subject of the remaining bust, unknown for many years, is James Oliver (Oliver Farm Equipment Company), a prominent manufacturer of steel plows in the mid-1800s. The first bust to occupy one of the niches was of John Deere (Deere & Company), a company still well known today. The subject of the other missing bust is unknown, as is whether a fourth bust ever existed. Scoates died in 1939 and may have never fully realized his concept of a "Hall of Fame." However, there is plenty of time to fill the empty niches with the likes of Cyrus Hall McCormick (International Harvester Company), Jerome Increase Case (J. I. Case Corporation), or persons important to today's industry.

On equal footing with the art in this room is the ceiling with its elaborate raised plaster ornament in silver and gold paints. The ceiling depicts the forces that fuel agriculture: the universe—sun, moon, clouds, stars, and planets. Below the ceiling are light troughs that provide indirect lighting mostly to the ceiling, with a little to the floor. While much of this elaborate artistic expression remains, some of it has been lost to overpainting on two occasions. The first overpainting occurred in 1952 when a contract was let by the university to repaint walls and ceilings in the lobbies and lecture rooms within this and other buildings of the Vosper era with an institutional green color. This green color can be found over most of the flat areas of the ceiling in the lobby and in the lecture room and has proven to be difficult to remove. Since then, the green areas of the ceiling have been repainted white.

This image (*below*) from Mosca's report on the historic finishes is of the original wall and ceiling finishes remaining on a pilaster and beam in the lobby at the entrance to the vestibule. These finishes were used throughout the lobby and in the lecture hall, except that the base coat in the lecture room was a tan color, rather than the aluminum flake paint used in the lobby. This technique can also still be seen in the Animal Industries and Administration Buildings. (Courtesy of Matthew J. Mosca, Historic Paint Finishes Consultant)

As part of the 2015 renovation project, a grant from the National Trust for Historic Preservation's Cynthia Woods Mitchell Fund for Historic Interiors was obtained with the assistance of the BAEN, the College of Architecture, and the Center for Heritage Conservation. The grant enabled a detailed analysis of the painted finishes and a conservation investigation in the lobby and the lecture room under the direction of Quimby McCoy Preservation Architecture, with Matthew J. Mosca of Baltimore, Maryland, and Stashka Starr of Staska Conservation of Dallas. The analysis revealed that the entire ceiling was first painted a silver color (using aluminum flake paint), over which an umber-colored glaze was applied and then wiped off of the raised areas to allow the silver color to shine through. The glaze was applied with a ragged or stippled technique, using a rag or a stippling brush, which resulted in an uneven application. This technique was commonly used in buildings of this and earlier periods to achieve a rich, Old World appearance and was particularly effective when combined with raised ornament where it makes the surface look like embossed leather. The walls of the room were also painted with this technique. After the glazing, certain features of the decoration were highlighted in gold paint (using a bronze powder paint that has oxidized to the greenish-brown color that is seen today). Other small moldings were accentuated in blue-green and deep red colors. It is not known who executed these finishes.

The image (*above*), taken in the 1950s, shows the connection between the rear wing's tractor environment and this highly decorated lecture room. The large opening at the back of the room provides ample space for large equipment to be driven directly onto the stage. At the center of the stage is the revolving and lifting platform. The historic image (*right*), taken in 1949, provides documentation for what the ceiling looked like, at least in black and white, but the walls and doors by the date of this photograph had been overpainted. Note the lighting at the ceiling, which is similar to that found in the Petroleum Engineering and Chemistry Buildings. (Courtesy of Department of Biological and Agricultural Engineering, College of Agriculture and Life Sciences, Texas A&M University)

Seen from the top of the room, the expanse of space is dramatic, as is the mural straight ahead. Second to the Chemistry Building's lecture room, perhaps the most impressive of all of Vosper's spaces, this room gets its dramatic effect from its silver, blue, and green stenciled ceiling. The lecture room is the only space in the building that has been restored, or mostly so, to its original appearance, thanks to some clever and persistent faculty and administrators who were able to wrangle funds from myriad sources. The restoration work included the re-creation of the elaborate and colorful ceiling; the stage area, including the revolving platform (nonfunctional); restoration of the terrazzo flooring and synthetic leather known as Russialoid doors; and some of the lighting. Seating was replaced, but one original seat was brought back to the room. The room's focal point, a silver-colored chandelier, was also restored. The reproduction of the historic ceiling was executed by Restoration Associates Ltd. of San Antonio, led by Elisa Jary Nieto and Clint Nieto under the direction of Vaughn Construction, construction manager. The small, lighted blackboards are original and the screen in the middle of the stage is retractable, so that a connection to the rear wing is still possible, although there is no heavy farming equipment in the building today.

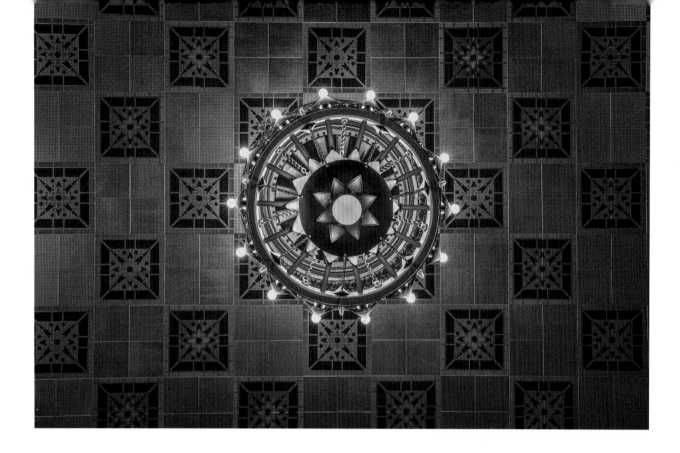

The chandelier (*above*) hangs in the center of the colorful stenciled ceiling and is composed of things you might find on the farm: a wagon wheel serves as the base for harrow teeth, shovels, disks, trace chains, and miscellaneous parts of farm machinery (*right*). Of course it is also painted with a silver color (aluminum flake paint), a whimsical treatment for such rudimentary elements. This is one of the most talked about features on tours of the building. The image above looking directly up shows how the star pattern in the ceiling tile is repeated in the chandelier.

Of all the decorative elements in the building, former students remember the mural most often, perhaps because it was a welcome distraction from the topic of the classroom or the vibrant colors and depiction of the history of agriculture in the state were simply appreciated for their own sake. The artist, Gertrude Babcock of Sonora, Texas, painted the mural between 1939 and 1940, a few years after the completion of the building. While the idea to add a mural came from Daniels Scoates, his successor, Fred R. Jones, completed the effort after Scoates died in 1939. Ms. Babcock was young for this assignment, having just graduated from the Texas State College for Women in Denton in 1933. She also attended the Academy of San Carlos in Mexico City, a national art school started in 1781 that taught modern-style painting, as opposed to classical European-style painting. Babcock was commissioned to create the mural by a large farming equipment manufacturer as a gift to the college. There are a total of six murals (including the ceiling mural that depicts the sky), each depicting a different period of agricultural history in Texas. This section, "Farming Practices—Early Days," shows the last generation's methods of using oxen and a wooden plow, without diversification of crops and with rows running downhill, contrary to soil conservation practices of today.

11

The Animal Industries Building and Horse Barn

DATE COMPLETED: Animal Industries: January 1934; Horse Barn: October 1933

COST: Animal Industries: $222,738.76; Horse Barn: $25,337.00

ARCHITECT: F. E. Giesecke (S. C. P. Vosper, designer)

CONTRACTOR: Animal Industries: H. E. Wattinger & Company;
Horse Barn: Walsh Burney and Key, Inc.

*"I remember when Harrison, one of the original designers came to visit the building.
He came in 1982 with his son. He was very old and his son explained that he wanted to see
the building because he felt it was one of the best buildings built."* [1]

—Barron Rector, 1998

UNTIL A CHANGE of tenancy and a recent renovation for air-conditioning, fire suppression systems, and life safety improvements that required some carefully integrated changes, this building was almost entirely as Vosper designed it, including furniture, office built-ins, aqua-colored toilet and sink ensembles, and a substantial amount of the elaborate decorative painting treatments that adorn the lobbies. It is still the only academic building where large areas of the original treatments can be seen, a reminder that all of these Depression-era buildings come with unexpected treasures. This may be the best and is definitely the last of Vosper's work on campus as he left town a couple of months before the building was completed.

History

Although the final payment for construction was made in January 1934, the building was not dedicated until December 10, 1936, as a memorial to the pioneer livestock men of Texas. Plans for a memorial were hatched in the early 1920s, and suitably, the Agricultural and Mechanical (A&M) College of Texas was selected for the site. But it was not until the early 1930s that the decision was made to use this building as the memorial. The front wing of the building is the most impressive and was first to be constructed. Soon after, the lecture room and an abattoir (a nice word for a slaughterhouse) were built on the back of the building. Prior to that, the Horse Barn, also designed by Vosper, was completed in a location just behind the building.

The first renovations were designed by Texas A&M System architect Henry D. Mayfield, Jr., in 1958 and 1970 for classroom improvements, including electrical and lighting changes. A fallout shelter was built within the abattoir during the 1960s but no longer remains, and air-conditioning was installed in the abattoir in 1963, one of the earlier buildings to get cooling on a list that included Cushing Library, Francis Hall, the Veterinary Hospital, and others. In 1976, Animal Sciences moved to the Kleberg Animal and Food Science Center on the West Campus, and soon after, Range Sciences moved into the building. The meat processing function remained in the abattoir until 1986 when it was moved to a Meat Science building next to the Kleberg Building. Around the same time, the Creamery, where

The front of this "memorial" as photographed in 1941 after the landscape had matured is extremely well done and almost festive in its design (*left*). The front and side views are tiered, like a wedding cake—a term that was applied to this architectural form after the stepping back of floors that responded to new zoning requirements in large cities like New York. At the cornice line, linked cattle skulls appear almost like frosting decoration. The rear view (*right*), photographed in 1936 during a judging class, illustrates how the front wing and the back wing are connected by the auditorium, at right. (Courtesy of Cushing Memorial Library and Archives, Texas A&M University)

students could buy milk and ice cream on campus, was also moved—to the dismay of many.

Few changes were made to the building during the years it was occupied by Range Sciences—now known as the Ecosystems Science and Management Department—which is why the building is so well preserved. A renovation to add a fire suppression system, address life safety code compliance issues, and replace air-conditioning equipment was completed in 2015 by Patterson Architects of Bryan, which was careful to preserve as much of the original building as possible. Despite the changes in use, including the latest tenant, Nuclear Engineering, the name of the building has not changed, and so far, neither has the incredible character of its interior.

The Horse Barn, built for the Animal Husbandry Department, was originally designed to include three phases of barns, but only the first phase was built. It did not take long for changes to come to this building as animals were moved away from the historic heart of the campus. In 1953, the barn was converted to office space for the editorial and publication departments of both the Texas Agricultural Experiment Station and the Extension Service at a cost of $64,000. A second conversion occurred in 1969 to the Forestry Science Department. The Experiment Station still uses the building as an annex.

Description

Four stories tall, this building is similar in form and style to the Agricultural Engineering Building that it faces across the planned Agricultural Quad. A cast stone water table forms the base; the first and second floors together form the body of the building, united by their spandrel panels; and the third floor acts as an attic story in that it is separated by a heavy belt course from the rest of the building. The fourth floor is set back from the rest of the façade and on top of that are two symmetrically placed penthouses, set back from the fourth floor. The *piano-nobile* is on the second floor.

The façade is arranged around a projecting cast stone entrance portico that features ornamental iron and glass doors and windows. Brick is the principal façade material with colorful Mexican tile used between windows of the first and second floors and in the cornice. The original steel casement windows have been replaced with aluminum. The wide belt course features the heads of rams and horses, while the cornice above the third floor features cattle skulls in the frieze that appear to support the cornice in the same way the owls do at the Agricultural Engineering Building, and with the same colorful patterned tile. The style is PWA Moderne with an extra dose of animal heads.

The form of the building is an H shape and, like Agricultural Engineering, is divided into three parts that correspond to the plan *parti*. The front wing facing the Quad houses the lobbies, administrative offices, and classrooms and laboratories, or the academic side of the industry. The short leg of the H is the two-story high auditorium. The rear wing, facing the Horse Barn, is the abattoir, designed for meat processing, or the practical side of the industry.

On the first floor is the entrance hall, which serves as a small lobby and connects to a corridor that runs nearly the length of the building off of which are classrooms. The floor is of colorful Mexican tile bordered in gray and green marble, and the walls have a gray marble wainscot with plaster above. The ceiling is flat with dropped beams and is trimmed with ornamental plaster moldings. The primary feature of the room is the grand stair that is found directly in front of the entrance. The stair, which splits at mid-floor level, takes the visitor to the *piano nobile* on the second floor, where another lobby called "Memorial Hall" is located. Off this hall, which has the same finishes as the first floor, are two entrances to the auditorium and an elaborately decorated library, as well as more classrooms and the department head's office. The grand stair is discontinued at this level. Smaller stairs and an elevator provide access to the third floor classrooms and laboratories. Originally, the top floor featured a small greenhouse on the west end and spaces designed for functions such as "Brooding" and feed storage, small animal laboratories, and a "Mature Fowl" room, all of which had doors leading to the outside roof deck. Extensive ventilation systems that exhausted through the roof were designed for the ceilings.

The auditorium at the center of the building is where the scientific study of animals meets slaughtering and meat processing. The two-story auditorium space has steeply stepped seating platforms facing a large stage area, with a connection to the abattoir. The stage was originally concrete with glazed hollow clay tile walls that were easy to clean as slaughtered animals were displayed during classes. The rest of the room was simple, in comparison to some of the other lecture rooms, with a wood wainscot and plaster walls, and the ceiling, which is a feature in other rooms, is labeled "color and decoration to be defined by architect" on the original architectural drawings. The original appearance of this ceiling is unknown. Windows are without stained glass. Due to the more utilitarian needs of the auditorium, the most elaborate space was the library, a long rectangular room that faces the Quad and is lined with wood bookshelves on the walls, an ornamental iron and glass partition, and a decorative ceiling, according to the drawings. The ceiling, however, does not appear to have been executed as planned, and when air-conditioning was added to the building in the 1960s, the mechanical room was located in the middle of this library space, essentially splitting the room in half and making a portion of the room inaccessible.

The Horse Barn, or "Horse Barns," as it was labeled on the drawings, was designed as a much larger complex of stables surrounding an exercising track, but only the front stable structure, called phase one, was built. The front door faced north and was located within a central taller section of the building flanked by lower wings housing the horse stalls. The entrance led into a lobby with two display stalls and built-in display cases, access to a tack room, and other functions. A spiral staircase led to an upper level that was fitted for grain and hay storage. The lobby connected to a central corridor that ran the length of the building with seven stalls on each side of each wing. The wings looked like stables, with regular openings and wood stall doors. The stalls on the south side were specially fitted as maternity stalls, a colt stall, tie stalls, and a cleaning alley that provided access to these stalls. Some of these details have changed in order to adapt the building for offices, but the essential character of the place on the exterior remains strong. The façades are clad in the same brick found on the other Vosper buildings with details in cast stone and Mexican tile, but used more sparingly. Among the best remembered features of this building are the two unique weathervanes.

The diagram of the Animal Industries Building on the left depicts the plan organization of the building—the *parti*—with emphasis on the public and most important spaces which lead to the auditorium. The diagram on the right illustrates the vertical arrangement of these same spaces, starting outside the building and into the auditorium.

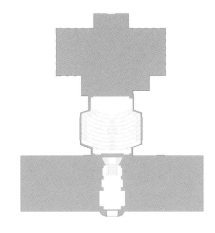

A two-story-high cast stone portico that protrudes from the façade and is decorated with ornament befitting an animal industries building, including a life-size horseshoe and nail molding that mimics a classical egg and dart molding accentuates the entrance. The portico features an ornamental iron and glass pendant light fixture and door grills. The original limestone porch steps were replaced in a recent renovation of the open space in front of the building that created an accessible entrance (*left*). The center door has been replaced with a modern-day storefront door; the original door remained stored in the building as of 2015. The window above the door is one of the only original windows left in the building. The photograph (*below*) shows the entrance as it appeared in 1947 with members of the Rodeo Club. (Courtesy of Cushing Memorial Library and Archives, Texas A&M University)

The ironwork within the entrance portico incorporates delicate traditional forms in combination with Texas cattle brands. Based on early photographs of the entrance, the ironwork appears to have been painted a uniform light color, but the colors and gold leaf accents of the Agricultural Engineering Building suggest there may have been more to this entrance originally. The finish on the interior of the doors is a special faux-bronze painted finish that is used on all of the ironwork of the entrance hall and the Hall of Fame above, and the frames are made of a hammered metal with a similar finish and rosettes, outlined with a rope molding.

Above the entrance is the shield designed by Vosper for Animal Industries that is flanked by a pair of cornucopia brimming with budding flowers that transition into rams' heads as they meet the ledge of the molding surrounding the entrance. The shield features the word *genetics* above an abstracted tree trunk with branches for six edible livestock. From top left moving clockwise is a cow, sheep, horse, chicken, goat, and pig.

On the façades of the building, one can find a wide variety of animal heads, including one that is commonly used in classical architecture called the *bucranium*, a word derived from the Latin "bos" for bovine and "cranium" for skull. There is a long tradition related to the use of *bucrania*; the origin of this decorative element is in a Greek and Roman ceremonial sacrifice involving the killing of an animal, a particularly appropriate choice here. In place of the traditional ox's skull here is a horse's skull used within the colorful Mexican tile of the spandrel panels, at left. The garland draped around the skull is also a part of the ceremonial ritual. At the belt course separating the second floor from the third floor are animal heads that include the horse and ram (right). At the cornice is the more traditional ox's skull, which is used in the same way that the owl's heads are used at the Agricultural Engineering Building to visually support the top of the cornice alternating with colorful patterned tile in the frieze.

The interior is also full of animal heads. The column and pilaster capitals here are completely transformed from classical columns to oversized animal groupings that appear to support the ceiling beams above them. Here are horse torsos along with heads of Texas Longhorn cattle and rams. Even the cove molding at the ceiling features cattle and hooves trimmed in rope. The painted finishes here are the original 1934 finishes for the entire ceiling in this building's entrance and lobby; the treatment is achieved by painting a base color and adding a glaze that is ragged or stippled to create this effect.

This monumental terrazzo stair leads from the entrance hall on the first floor to the "Memorial Hall" on the second floor (*left*). This elaborate stair is part of the processional experience to reach the most important rooms of the building on the second floor—the auditorium and library. The small medallions on the edge of the stair and along the side of the second floor feature the "portraits" of eight different animals (*right*). The newel post is reserved for the noble ram's head.

The stair railing creatively uses intertwined rope and barbwire to create the balusters. The railing is made of metal with a special painted finish that has partially worn off and has a wood handrail.

The floor tile in this and other Vosper buildings is defined on the architectural drawings as a "Mexican Cement Tile" and is a product with a long history of use around the world. However, closer to home Vosper would have known it from his study of old Spanish missions and from his travels to Mexico and southern Texas. Sometimes referred to as *encaustic* tile for the method of introducing pigment thought a wax vehicle, this material was used in Texas most commonly in the latter half of the nineteenth century. The patterns that can be created with this material are infinite. The tile can also be used on walls, as Vosper used it on the interior of the Central Christian Church in Austin. The same material can be used outside, but the exposure to sun does fade it somewhat, and exposure to foot traffic wears down the surface over time. This material has a long life and is practical; it is also enjoying a bit of a renaissance and is marketed as "concrete tile" today.

The ironwork introduced on the stair railing continues on the second floor in the elaborate doors and windows that lead to the library. The design of these doors is similar to those of the entrance and feature more cattle brands. The metal is hammered and the finish is a faux bronze; these special finishes remain in good condition. On the inside of the library is another iron and glass partition that was relocated within the room when a mechanical room was built in the middle of the space. The space is now used as a conference room on both sides of the mechanical room. A similar iron and glass partition was used in the Administration Building, also with a faux-bronze finish. Note the simple but delicate door latch on the left-hand door.

Charming details like this perforated sheet copper over stained glass remain on the partition in the library.

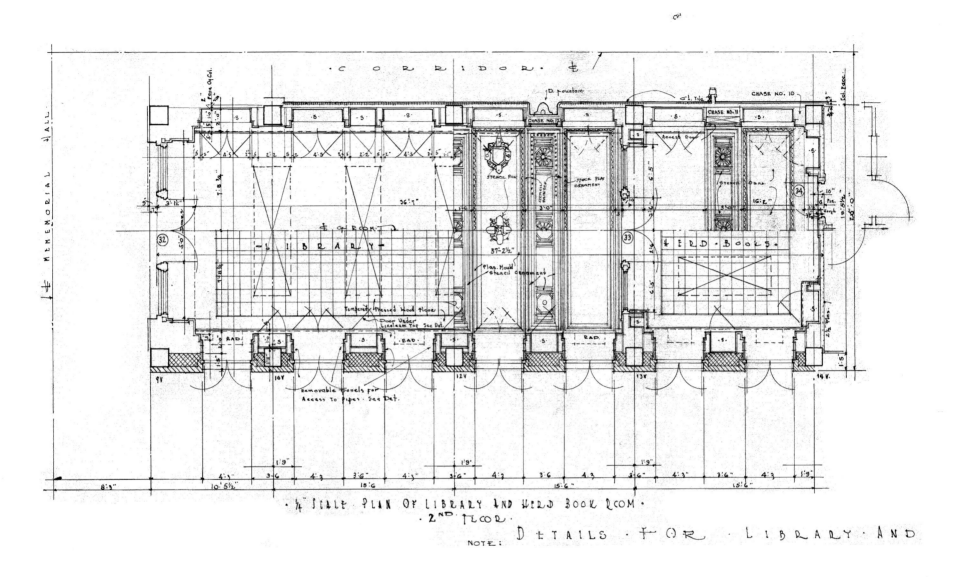

·4" SCALE PLAN OF LIBRARY AND HERD BOOK ROOM·
·2ND FLOOR·

DETAILS · FOR · LIBRARY · AND

NOTE:

The floor plan for the library provides an indication of the level of decoration that was provided for this space. As was typical at the time, the floor plan is shown with a reflected ceiling plan on one-half of the plan. This was done in part to enable the designer and the builder to visually understand how the floor and ceiling worked together and in part to save the architect from having to draw the entire plan twice. The drawing of both floor and ceiling is a tradition with a long past and was also part of the *Beaux-Arts* tradition, but is rarely done today. This drawing was made and traced by Raiford L. Stripling. (Copyright 2016 Texas A&M University)

The auditorium in this building was designed for the presentation of animals, both dead and alive. Hung from the ceiling was a rail on which hooks were used to support animal carcasses for display purposes that ran from the abattoir into the auditorium and then back. Remnants of this rail system remain within the former abattoir. The remainder of the auditorium has the same steep stepped seating as the other lecture rooms of the era, but the decoration is simpler. The small door on stage to the left of the chalkboard is the original connection to the rear wing, except that the original door nearly reached the ceiling. The front doors to the room are wood covered in the same synthetic leather knows as Russialoid found in the other lecture rooms, but this might have been the place to use real cowhide.

This historic image shows the auditorium in use for teaching purposes. The longhorn cattle heads adorning the walls may be a Vosper touch. (Courtesy of Cushing Memorial Library and Archives, Texas A&M University)

The largest ranches in Texas were invited to brand the wood in the office of the department head. Designed with the theme of early ranch homes, the floors are a mosaic of broken stone, and the walls are paneled in chestnut wood. One wall has full height wood paneling with hidden doors leading to storage cabinets, the hall, and a private restroom. The ceiling is, as usual, the star of the room, featuring faux-wood beams with half-round wood logs and smaller wood lattice depicting a traditional *viga* and *latilla* laid in a chevron pattern. Each of the Vosper buildings had, and many still have, a department head office of distinction, usually treated with a special theme related to the rest of the building. These are unique spaces, typically with an accompanying unique private restroom featuring bright-colored tiles and equally colorful plumbing fixtures.

The function of the Horse Barn has moved to a far more sophisticated equine facility that has recently opened. According to the TAMU Animal Science Department, Texas is home to more than one million horses, or 15 percent of all horses nationwide. This was, and still is, a vital part of animal science education and research. Vosper's barn design is simpler than that of his academic buildings but still incorporates the same brick, cast stone, and Mexican tile; it even has its own *cartouche*, or seal, above the entrance (*right*).

This interior view of the lobby shows that even in a stable, a touch of ornamental ironwork was used to make the building special and to describe its purpose. The door leads to one of the two "display stalls." The small window on the right was one of the "display cases." Records of the interiors of all of Vosper's buildings are scarce and difficult to find because they are often catalogued under someone's name or an event, rather than with the building. This particular image is catalogued according to the name of the photographer, W. E. Brown Jr., but an analysis of the architectural drawings made it possible to identify its location within the Horse Barn. (Courtesy of Cushing Memorial Library and Archives, Texas A&M University)

The two weathervanes that are currently located on the flanking lower wings of the Horse Barn were originally paired on the top of the central, taller section of the building. During one of the renovations of the building, they were either moved or replaced with replica weathervanes in new locations. The weathervane on the east wing (*left*), depicts a cowboy preparing to rope a rabbit in a cactus patch, and on the west wing (*right*), a cowboy trying to control a horse that is bucking at a snake in the grass. These metal creations are a charming piece of craftsmanship that is often remembered by former students. In fact, if one were describing Vosper's buildings in a word, it would have to be "memorable."

The Victorian Barracks – Ross Hall, 1891 – 1955

Ross Hall, originally called the "Barracks," was one of the early dormitories on campus. This building, like those before it, was built of cherry-red brick and in the Victorian style, with steep roofs, wraparound balconies, and plenty of decoration. Despite the elaborate exterior, the interior contained large, plain rooms with bare walls. The forty-one rooms in Ross Hall were heated with wood-burning stoves, but this was one of the few amenities. Not until 1910 was the building equipped with a hot water heating system and bathing facilities, soon followed. Like Foster Hall, this building was leveled brick by brick so that the brick could be sold and reused.

"I have this morning assumed charge of the A. & M. C. So far as I can tell, my presence is very acceptable to all parties and a short talk made [to] the young men this morning seemed to take very well . . . . I find the work in the details somewhat annoying, but not difficult, & I will soon have things running smoothly here. I think I shall like it . . ."

12

The Campus Today

BALANCING GROWTH AND HERITAGE

The End of an Era

S. C. P. VOSPER'S departure from the campus at the end of 1933 marked the end of an era. Each of the ten major buildings he designed remain to demonstrate his mastery of classical form, his skill in detailed design, his profound knowledge of materials and finishes, and his ability to infuse his designs with elements that spoke eloquently about the agricultural and engineering activity present on the campus. F. E. Giesecke, the college architect who established the underlying plan of the campus in 1910, had joined forces with Frederick W. Hensel, Jr., the Head of the Landscape Art Department, to reorient the campus to the new entrance from Highway 6, allowing the last of Vosper's buildings to shape the civic spaces in this eastern expansion. The availability of funds and highly skilled labor during the Depression gave Vosper's genius full rein, and the Animal Industries Building was the last, and arguably the most mature, of his extraordinarily memorable designs for the college.

The late 1930s would bring fundamental changes to the institution. Enrollment, that stayed around 2,000 in the last decade of the nineteenth century, had reached 6,000 by 1939, requiring the construction of fourteen new dormitory buildings, twelve of them to the south of the expanded campus to house the Corps of Cadets. While they followed the campus pattern of brick structures with classically proportioned punched openings, Houston architect Albert Finn used a PWA Moderne architectural style, using two contrasting shades of brick and sections of brick with vertical fluting (page 209). In the same year, the board of directors, anticipating a need for space for more academic buildings, resolved that faculty houses would no longer be permitted on campus. Land to the south and east of the campus was being developed for new subdivisions, and faculty homes were either moved to new locations or demolished.[1] In 1938, facing annexation by the city of Bryan, a group of faculty proposed to charter the college community as an independent city. The vote to incorporate passed 217 to 39.[2] The founders anticipated that the new city of College Station would develop as a dormitory community for the campus, allowing the residents to continue an institutional village lifestyle, with Bryan, the seat of county government, providing primary mercantile and entertainment support.[3] Time would prove them wrong!

Meanwhile, world events could not be ignored on a campus that was all male, all military, and that had already demonstrated its dedication to duty in the first global conflict. With the entry of the United States into World War II the student population had dropped from 6,544 in 1942 to 2,205 by 1943. Brazos County became home to the Bryan Army Air Base in 1942, and coursework in electrical and radio engineering was streamlined to train students in the emerging technologies to support the war effort.[4]

In 1945, with the war in Europe over, and the battles in the Pacific coming to an end, the college architect, by then seventy-six years old, retired to the Giesecke family homestead in New Braunfels. From the time of his graduation in 1886, Frederick Giesecke had quite literally shaped the physical form of the campus. In his first twenty-six years, he proposed the plan for the campus that endures to this day, designed or oversaw the construction of eighteen major buildings, engineered both structural and mechanical systems for many of those buildings, and designed the service infrastructure of the campus. After his return from Austin in 1927, joined two years later by S. C. P. Vosper, whose work has been described in the previous chapters, he continued to guide and direct every aspect of campus growth. However, in the last pages of his self-effacing autobiography, completed just hours before a fatal heart attack on June 27, 1953, Giesecke reflected mainly on his series of textbooks on mechanical drawing, the department he headed at age 19, and the F. Paul Anderson Medal from the American Society of Heating and Ventilating Engineers that he received in 1941. He notes, somewhat laconically, "after leaving A&M College I continued my professional work at New Braunfels as well as I could with the limited means available."[5] His visible legacy is the campus, albeit little acknowledged, except for being named an

The campus from the east circa 1940. Vosper's buildings sit in a relatively open landscape, defining large quadrangles within the eastern expansion. The 1939 dormitories and new dining hall to the south created their own series of courtyards. Faculty housing would go from the campus by the end of World War II. (Courtesy of Cushing Memorial Library and Archives, Texas A&M University)

Outstanding Alumnus by the College of Architecture in 2004, and the Engineering Research Building completed in 2015 that carries his name.

After World War II and the G. I. Bill

Thanks to the G. I. Bill and the Aggie reputation for practical education, the year following World War II saw enrollment leap to nearly 9,000 students. Space on the pre-war campus was overwhelmed, and freshmen students were housed and taught at the former Bryan Army Air Base.[6] The 1950s saw a building boom to accommodate new programs and more students, with buildings sited in general accordance with the Geisecke plan, taking advantage of the area cleared of faculty houses, and the land available toward Highway 6.

In the absence of Giesecke's guiding hand, while buildings responded to the academic, administrative, recreational, and social programmatic needs of the users, their appearance reflected the current stylistic trends embraced by the designers, often paying scant attention to the character of the buildings that surrounded them.

The 1950 Biological Sciences Building, designed by architect Carleton Adams and built by the J. W. Bateson Company, adopted some Modern characteristics, with thin concrete cantilevered eyebrows over the windows, although it maintained the campus tradition of cast stone surrounds at the main entrances. The use of an individual style continued with a 1967 addition for biological sciences by architects and engineers Pitts Mebane Phelps & White of Beaumont that provided a strong contrast with the earlier building. The structural columns and floor plates are expressed by a white concrete grid on the façade, with thin vertical windows separated by plain brick panels in the now-standard buff tone. The contractors were Lockwood Andrews Newman of Houston.

The contrasting appearance of the 1950 and 1967 Biological Sciences Buildings follows the stylistic trends of contemporary published work. While the scale of the buildings maintained that of the historic campus, their architecture contrasted with surrounding buildings. (Photograph by Marcel Erminy)

The 1951 Richard Coke Building was designed by Herbert Voelker & Associates, Architects, and built by the Fisher Construction Company, to house the president and administration of the college. Langford describes it as "the most elegantly finished building on the campus."[7] The exterior used a restrained Beaux-Arts style with narrow salmon-pink brick walls with Indiana limestone for the base and belt courses. The interior used marble walls, terrazzo floors, and mahogany paneling, materials and finishes whose quality Vosper would have appreciated.

In the same year, the Memorial Student Center (MSC) replaced the YMCA as the social center of the campus, built as a memorial to the 844 former students who had given their lives in service to their country. Architect Carleton Adams was influenced by the Prairie Style architecture of Frank Lloyd Wright, using long, narrow blocks of Texas limestone contrasted by strips of metal-framed windows and deep horizontal bands of white concrete on the exterior. While a relatively large building, filling an entire block formerly occupied by faculty homes, the MSC achieved a residential scale, largely two stories in height, and depressing a three-story west end with a half-basement. Built by the R. E. McKee Construction Company, the MSC took over two years to build and cost in excess of $2 million.

The MSC supplanted all the social activities formerly found in the YMCA, and in 1958, the All Faiths Chapel ended the YMCA's spiritual purpose. Architecture professor Dik Vrooman won the design competition for the chapel, marking the last time a serving faculty member would design a building for the campus. Like Adams, Vrooman was influenced by Prairie style design, using strong horizontal lines, with the exterior Texas limestone walls flowing into the interiors separated only by frameless glass panels, allowing the play of light and the texture of the materials to provide visual interest. The delicate geometry of the subtle stained glass in the building also draws on Wright as a precedent.

"Aspirations" Become Reality

The rapid growth and changing societal patterns of the 1950s created significant discord between faculty and administration, and between students and faculty. The requirement for most students to be members of the Corps of Cadets and the prohibition on female enrollment were at the root of the troubles.[8] James Earl Rudder, a hero of the D-Day landing at Omaha Beach, and whose post-war service at the Texas General Land Office had resulted in major reforms aimed at transparency and

Carleton Adams's design for the Memorial Student Center was clearly influenced by the horizontality of Frank Lloyd Wright's Prairie Style residential architecture, appropriate for a structure often referred to as the "living room of the campus." (Courtesy of Cushing Memorial Library and Archives, Texas A&M University)

In keeping with its Modernist style, the form of the 1963 Architecture Building reflects it function. The exterior used brick on the lower level, with thin slabs of travertine marble on the east and west sides of the upper elevations, and glass curtain walls for the studios, shaded by tinted glass screens hung on the north and south. The simple forms relied on the play of light on the lower courtyard walls, the external columns, and recessed entrances, to provide interest. (Courtesy of Cushing Memorial Library and Archives, Texas A&M University)

fairness for veterans' rights, was appointed as the twenty-first president of the college in 1959. Dethloff reports that, despite his military and governmental success, the Texas native who had earned his degree in Agriculture from Texas Agricultural and Mechanical (A&M) College in 1932, was not expected to bring any significant change to the institution.[9]

Rudder, however, had built his career on achieving the unexpected. With the college's centennial less than twenty years away, Rudder called on faculty, students, and staff to suggest a future for the college in an "Aspirations Study."[10] The Century Council also developed a report, and the board of directors compiled a "Blueprint for Progress," published in 1962. Each document recognized the need for bold changes. Rudder asked the state legislature to change the name of the institution to Texas A&M University, established the Corps of Cadets as a voluntary program, and allowed females to enroll, initially on a limited basis due to lack of housing. On the academic front, he encouraged the development of five new colleges, Education, Liberal Arts, Science, Geosciences, and Architecture, recognizing that if A&M was to be a true university it must be far more than "agricultural and mechanical" in nature. However, the centennial reports had all recognized that the original agricultural and

engineering disciplines provided essential foundations for the Land Grant College, and that the traditions and values that had developed since 1876 defined unique qualities of which A&M was rightly proud.[11]

The first of the new colleges to receive its own building was Architecture. The 1963 building was designed by Harwood K. Smith & Partners of Dallas. Smith was a member of the first class of graduates of the five-year bachelor of architecture program in 1936, and his firm, later HKS Inc., would design a second architecture building a decade later. The building was initially three-stories in height, though designed to receive a fourth floor that would be added some fifteen years later. The simple plan housed administrative offices, a library, and a 200-seat auditorium on the lower level, with two floors of faculty offices and design studios above, supported by exposed reinforced concrete columns. The studio floors used a pinwheel plan form allowing corridors to extend to the exterior walls, providing informal gathering spaces to foster cross-disciplinary learning. Caudill Rowlett Scott (CRS) had used this approach in the design of Larson Hall at Radcliff College in Cambridge, though sadly the lounges were lost at A&M when the hallways were enclosed to create needed office space.

By 1970, the university had grown to more than 14,000 students, including many females and a significant number of graduate students. Earl Rudder, perhaps the greatest change-agent in the institution's history, died after a brief illness in March 1970. He was succeeded as president by Jack K. Williams, a former Marine, distinguished historian, and experienced administrator, well-versed in the Texas political process, who would continue the transformation from college to university with a more academic emphasis.

Planning for the Future

The architectural firm CRS was established in College Station while Bill Caudill and John Rowlett were on the faculty. A&M graduates Willie Pena '42 and Wallie Scott '43 became founding partners after service in World War II. In 1958, the firm moved to Houston and rapidly developed an international reputation. The university turned to them to examine the physical organization of the campus and make recommendations for future growth. Their *Preliminary Campus Plan and Environmental Guidelines* was published in 1970, projecting a student population of 20,000 by 1978.[12] The document suggested some building design guidelines, following the precepts of functionality and energy conservation for which the firm was known, but the input to the study was not sufficiently visionary, and the plan was never implemented. By 1978 the actual enrolment had exceeded 30,000. In the absence of a clearly defined campus plan, physical changes continued to be made based on expediency and academic politics.

President Williams' first construction priority was dormitories for the rapidly growing female enrollment. Then, in accordance with the recommendations of the "Aspirations" reports to increase the visibility of the arts, he initiated the construction of properly designed auditoria for music and theater and a central facility for conferences and meeting rooms. This was achieved by demolishing Guion Hall, the 1918 assembly building with its inflexible and outdated space, and constructing a new building with three professionally equipped auditoria and a large first floor exhibit space. The theater complex was flanked by a twelve-story

tower with office and meeting spaces, whose top floors housed a Faculty Club (now the University Club) that provided excellent views over the campus. Dallas architects Jarvis Putty Jarvis, Inc. designed the J. Earl Rudder Center in 1972. Some exterior surfaces have bush-hammered concrete ribs, a technique first used by architect Paul Rudolph in his 1963 Architecture Building at Yale, contrasted with white concrete surfaces and large areas of glass. The courtyard between the Rudder Center and the Memorial Student Center continues to serve as a major campus gathering space, enhanced by a large water feature.

Like its predecessor Guion Hall, the uditoria building of the 1972 Rudder Center provides the south terminus to Military Walk, and serves as a backdrop to the life-size statue of James Earl Rudder' 32, A&M's influential twenty-first president, in whose memory the center is dedicated. (Photograph by Marcel Erminy)

Pressure for space, and the desire to remain close to the center of campus led to the addition of other vertical buildings, while at the same time a historic landmark tower was being lost. The removal of Vosper's magnificent tower on the Geology and Petroleum Engineering Building in 1972, discussed in chapter six, was deemed necessary for structural reasons. The loss of this iconic landmark attracted negative comments in the campus newspaper, but it was not long before other "towers" appeared. In 1973, the College of Liberal Arts received new classrooms and office space with the construction of the M. T. Harrington Buildings on the north side of the quadrangle bounded by the Academic Building on the west and Cushing Library on the east. Each used sloped and corbelled brickwork, a style totally alien to the adjacent classical buildings, the only continuity being provided by the ubiquitous buff-colored brick. The twelve-story Rudder Tower, the first new vertical feature on campus other

than the water tower, had been sited well to the south of the west-east axis of Giesecke's plan, and provided an appropriate landmark for the social and cultural centers of the campus without affecting the visual scale of the three- to four-story historic campus. In 1974, there was discussion about demolishing the historic Cushing Library to replace it with a library tower, but happily, the idea was not pursued.[13] Nevertheless, the campus continued to grow upward on the periphery of the historic core, with new buildings for Civil Engineering and the Texas Transportation Institute in 1987, and for Petroleum Engineering in 1989. Each of these buildings used its own design vocabulary, the color palette of the materials providing the only visual connection to the rest of the campus.

However, the scale of the 1930s east quadrangle proposed in the Giesecke-Hensel plan, and bounded by three of Vosper's buildings, Scoates Hall, the Administration Building, and the

The density of the historic campus was increased by the tower structures constructed between 1972 and 1987 and, with the exception of the Oceanography and Meteorology Building and the Harrington Tower, both added in 1973, the new buildings did not disturb the scale of the historic core of the campus. (Courtesy of Cushing Memorial Library and Archives, Texas A&M University)

The addition of the 1973 Oceanography and Meteorology Building not only changed the scale of the quadrangle established as a part of the eastern expansion of the campus, but unbalanced the critical symmetry of the view from New Main Drive. (Photograph by Marcel Erminy)

Animal Industries Building, and by E. B. La Roche's 1922 Agriculture Building, was forever disrupted by the fifteen-story Oceanography and Meteorology Building constructed in 1973.

Design Without Context

Adelsperger's 1916 Hospital Building had been designed to serve 700 students, and even though it boasted bathroom facilities on every floor, it was long out of date. Its function was replaced by the Beutel Health Center, constructed to the north of the YMCA Building in 1973. The increasing number of women on campus even prompted the hiring of a female physician. The building's appearance was driven by the need for privacy, resulting in a fortress-like exterior. The lack of connection with pedestrian traffic would have been more noticeable had Military Walk been preserved for its cultural significance, but with the construction of the 1939 dormitories and Duncan Dining

The form of the 1977 Langford Architecture Building, seen here from the east quad, shows the studio floors set back as a series of trays. The interior has an open atrium along the central spine, with offices arranged along the west side, a sectional form that resembles Harvard Graduate School of Design's Gund Hall. The Zachry Engineering Building was also in a Brutalist style, although the major expansion begun in 2015 stripped the building to its steel frame, leaving the Langford Building as one of a few examples of Brutalism on the campus. (Photograph by Marcel Erminy)

Hall on the south side of campus, the cadets no longer marched along it to assembly and mess. As a result, during the "pedestrianization" of the central campus in the early 1970s, the street that had been at the heart of campus life for six decades was re-imagined as a green strip interspersed with inaccessible crossings and defensive-looking, bush-hammered concrete kiosks plastered with unsightly notices.

This was the end-period of so-called "Brutalist" architecture in the United States, a style that used large areas of raw concrete to create structures that generally seemed heavy and often unwelcoming, and rarely favored by the public. Both the 1972 Zachry Engineering Building and the 1977 building designed to accommodate the expanding College of Architecture, used heavy precast concrete systems. The Architecture Building, placed across the east quadrangle from the fifteen-story Oceanography and Meteorology tower, did at least maintain the height limitation established by its earlier neighbors, Vosper's Scoates Hall and the Administration Building. However, it encroached on the street lines laid out by Giesecke and Hensel by extending its lower level into the East Quad. HKS, Inc. of Dallas, continued the Brutalist style on the interior by exposing the structural and mechanical systems, using the building as an educational tool for its occupants. The large concrete components were precast in Dallas, and were assembled like a gigantic Lego set.

Repairing an Icon: Rethinking Values

By now, the student population had exceeded 30,000, and pressure for new classroom and faculty office space was intense. New construction required long-term preparation, and attention turned to repurposing existing spaces and the growing issues of deferred maintenance and accessibility.

During the same years that the Rudder administration was developing goals for the future of Texas A&M, the nation had been looking backward in preparation for the Bicentennial of the United States. Part of the celebrations were to focus on the sites and places associated with the events of the late eighteenth century, and architects, engineers, and conservators from the National Park Service and in private practice developed "best practices" for the treatment of historic properties. The National Historic Preservation Act of 1966 and the "Standards" published subsequent to it provided guidance to work aimed at the preservation and reuse of existing buildings. Often described in medically related terminology, the process encouraged the development of a thorough history in order to identify the authentic nature of the building, followed by an analysis of later changes and defects, and undertaking selected diagnostic tests, before prescribing the proper course of treatment. While it would be some years before the university formally adopted such processes, certain administrators had an inherent "feel" for the significance of aspects of the campus heritage.

By 1980, the Academic Building, constructed in 1914 and long accepted as the iconic center of the campus, was showing significant signs of weathering, and portions of the cast stone cornice were cracked and in danger of falling. Also, its Beaux-Arts design meant that the building was approached on all sides up a series of steps, making access difficult for some users.

In initiating work for new construction, or to make changes to existing buildings, the University System called for a user coordinator, generally an administrator housed in the building. In 1983, the Academic Building was fortunate to have Jerry Gaston, then head of the Sociology Department, in that role. After spending two years as a graduate student at Yale, he recognized that, as Sir Winston Churchill famously said, "we shape our buildings, and then our buildings shape us."[14] Tim Donathen, a 1974 A&M architecture graduate who rose through the ranks in the Texas A&M University System's Office of Facilities Planning and Construction between 1980 and 2006, was also sympathetic to the significance of built heritage, and supported the reuse of existing buildings wherever possible.[15]

Austin architect Chartier Newton '56 was engaged to examine the Academic Building and prepare plans for an exterior renovation that would include providing ramped access to its main level. The copper dome was a particular problem, due in no small part to collateral damage caused by cadets attempting to shoot out a light bulb that shone atop the dome in the

The northwest bay of the Academic Building as the original white-painted wood windows were being replaced. While there was an attempt to match the window proportions in the new aluminum frames, the decision to replace the white-painted, double-hung sashes with their small glass panes by aluminum frames with a dark bronze finish and large sheets of tinted glass, effectively produces a blank look, totally changing the original appearance. (Photograph by David Woodcock)

1920s! Newton, familiar with the new preservation standards, proposed in-kind repair of all the cast stone elements, and fully refurbishing the copper dome. The new sections of stone and brick were blended into the original materials by the use of organic patination, a process that applied liquid cow manure to the surfaces. Needless to say, this caused significant comment in the Austin newspapers, but it proved highly successful, as did Newton's addition of two shallow ramps to the north and south of the west entrance, that were flanked by cast stone balustrades. The details of the balustrade were copied from Samuel Gideon's second floor balcony, a philosophical approach that ensured that the addition would be in harmony with the original design. Gideon's beautifully designed, white-painted wood windows caused the building to sparkle, especially in the setting sun, and Newton's proposal to repair and repaint the 1914 windows was recommended by the System Office of Facilities Planning and Construction, and strongly supported by the Board of Regents. While the cost of cyclical maintenance of painted surfaces is significant, the aesthetic of many classical buildings depends on the visual relationship between materials and surfaces, and in this case, the underlying windows were in good condition, needing only minor repair to the glass putty and the paint coating. The outcome of the 1983 work demonstrated that heritage buildings could be brought back to life. Sadly, the will to maintain the building was lacking, and only ten years later the Academic Building was subjected to the same fate as most of the other historic buildings on campus, and its cypress wood windows with delicate glass panes were replaced by bronze aluminum frames filed with large sheets of dark glass, creating an "empty" appearance.[16]

Preservation Education

The changing administrative perspective on the treatment of historic buildings was paralleled by the development of an academic focus on historic preservation based in the College of Architecture. Instruction in the detailed recording of historic structures began in 1977, using the model of the National Park Service's Historic American Buildings Survey (HABS). After several years of nationally recognized contributions to the HABS collection in the Library of Congress, the Historic Resources Imaging Laboratory was established in 1991 to integrate the emerging use of computer technology into the measuring and drawing process. Courses in historic building technology, preservation theory and planning, and landscape preservation followed, leading to the approval of a university-wide, cross-disciplinary graduate Certificate in Historic Preservation in 1995. The certificate drew the attention of graduate students in engineering, agriculture and liberal arts, as well as each of the disciplines in the College of Architecture, and in 2005, the research unit received the Regent's approval as the Center for Heritage Conservation. The title recognized that conservation and sustainability have a direct connection in the wise use of resources.

Growing student participation led to an increased awareness of the significance of the campus buildings. Using the campus as a classroom, they examined the qualities of buildings that were barely noticed, and documented the roads and open spaces that established the framework for the campus. The university, long dedicated to the heritage of its intangible traditions, began to value the buildings, places, and spaces as important tangible heritage.

Recognizing Built Heritage

Once again the growth in enrollment, particularly at the graduate and professional levels, and the concomitant increase in research activity in all disciplines, posed extraordinary pressure on space. The Texas Coordinating Board for Higher Education establishes standards for academic space, and the College Station campus was found to be a million square feet short! Under President William Mobley, the Committee on Facilities Planning and Construction (CFPC), chaired from 1986 by Vice Provost for Administration Jerry Gaston, an examination of space use on the central campus was made, and nonacademic functions were moved off the central campus and space reassigned for teaching and research purposes. In addition to Gaston, the CFPC included mathematics professor Bill Perry, first as dean of faculties and later as executive associate provost. Perry had grown up with a

love of old buildings, recognizing their value to his student experience at the University of Illinois, and had taught in several historic buildings since coming to A&M. Their policy was to reuse and repurpose existing buildings wherever possible. While new academic space using Permanent University Fund (PUF) monies required long-term planning, support spaces could be rehabilitated using revenue bonds.

By 1995, Sbisa Dining Hall was in serious need of upgrading to meet code and energy efficiency standards. Once again, the value of the original design was recognized, and partitions and dropped ceilings were removed, recapturing the grand spaces created by Giesecke and Samuel Gideon in 1913. In recent years, the redevelopment of the paving in front of Sbisa has created a more authentic setting for the building.

As work to Sbisa was in the planning phase, Ray Bowen, a 1958 mechanical engineering graduate, became president of the university. Like Earl Rudder, Bowen wished to establish goals for the university's future, and worked with his businessman classmate, Jon Hagler, to initiate the VISION 2020 study. The charge to the 250-person task force was to examine all facets of the university's life, and establish imperative goals that would lead the university to be ranked in the top ten public institutions of higher education by 2020. For the first time, creating excellence through the physical form of the campus was included in the study. Under the heading, "Enrich Our Campus," the eighth imperative called for a "campus . . . conducive to scholarly work and study," achieved through, "innovative planning and bold leadership . . . (that will) attain the same pedestrian-friendly scale and green space that gives the Main Campus its character."[17]

As the university was approaching its 125th anniversary, grant funds were made available to each academic college to propose a celebratory activity. The College of Architecture proposed drawing attention to the built heritage of the campus through the addition of historic markers. The Campus Remembered project used a student and faculty team to survey the core of the campus, markers were designed and wording agreed, and bronze plaques installed on the selected buildings. In September 2002, newly appointed University President Bob Gates unveiled the marker on Vosper's Administration Building, by then named for

The dedication of the historic marker on Vosper's Administration Building provided an opportunity to celebrate the architectural heritage of the campus. The occasion was also marked by the meeting of architect Preston Geren Jr., FAIA, the grandson of College Architect F. E. Giesecke (left in photograph) and Bob Fretz Sr. and Bob Fretz Jr., the son and grandson of Edmond A. Fretz, who had founded the Standard Construction Co., the contractor for the building (right in photograph). Soon after the Administration Building was complete, the contracting firm was renamed Fretz Construction, the name it still uses. (Courtesy of College of Architecture, Texas A&M University)

past president Jack K. Williams. There were sixteen other markers at that time, causing some to suggest that the campus only had seventeen significant buildings, but the number was based solely on the budgetary limitation of the Campus Remembered grant, leaving many important historic structures unmarked.

Implementing Campus Enrichment

Prior to the arrival of Robert M. Gates as president of what had become a Land Grant, Sea Grant, Space Grant, Tier One Research University with nearly 45,000 students, president Bowen and his vice president for facilities, Chuck Sippial, had initiated a professionally developed Campus Master Plan. The commission was awarded to the Austin-based firm of Barnes, Gromatsky, Kosarek Architects, with Michael Dennis & Associates from Cambridge, Massachusetts. The year-long study involved the entire university community—students, faculty and staff—and resulted in a document that addressed the history of the campus, and offered a vision for the future based on a dense, pedestrian-oriented campus that reflected the same "sense of place" found

at the historic core of Giesecke's 1910 plan. The plan identified buildings of historic significance, including those marked in 2002. The document also included a Landscape Plan and an Architectural Plan, each of which established clear principles for new and remedial design. The Architectural Principles in the Campus Master Plan were based on the Beaux-Arts tradition used by Gideon and Vosper. Indeed, the principles for the design of façades, entrances, identity, and variety are illustrated using samples from their work.[18]

Overseeing the Campus Master Plan

The 2004 Campus Master Plan also called for the appointment of a university architect/campus planner and a Design Review Board (DRB) as "the guardian of campus development . . . to monitor and ensure that all design projects comply with the intent of the Campus Master Plan; to interpret the plan and guidelines; to grant exceptions when appropriate; and to recommend modifications or development of the Campus Master Plan as required," and "to evaluate projects to ensure that they meet the highest qualitative standards."[19] The plan was formally adopted by the board of regents, marking the first time in nearly a century that a physical plan for the campus and its buildings was supported at that level. In addition to his personal support of the Campus Master Plan, President Gates initiated a plan to increase the involvement of faculty, staff, and students in university decision-making through a number of advisory councils. One of these, the Council for the Built Environment (CBE), was charged to make recommendations on changes to the physical campus, and to oversee implementation of the Campus Master Plan. Also, J. Thomas Regan, dean of the College of Architecture, was appointed to chair a DRB composed of senior staff in the Office of Physical Plant and Design; planning, landscape, and design-focused faculty; the university archivist; a student senate member; and student representation from the graduate student council and from the American Institute of Architecture Students.

Recreating Military Walk

One of the first major projects to be generated by the new Campus Master Plan was drawn from a recommendation that Michael Dennis had based on a guide to the campus structure developed for instructional use, namely the re-instatement of the historic Military Walk as a major pedestrian path.[20] The concept to make Military Walk a record of the history and values of the A&M College of Texas was developed by EDAW/AECOM with Nancy McCoy, FAIA, of Quimby McCoy Preservation Architecture as historical consultant. The walk from Sbisa Dining Hall to the Rudder Center, originally a muddy path named Abilene Street, was now flanked on both sides by magnificent Live Oak trees, the result of Frederick Hensel's landscape improvements. The recreation of a walk wide enough to accommodate a corps march required a sophisticated irrigation system to protect the trees. Adjacent to the walk, a series of historic panels describe

Military Walk has not only assumed its former significance as a major pedestrian corridor, but it has become a campus showpiece. The dedication on September 27, 2010, marked the first time that the Corps of Cadets had marched down Military Walk in over fifty years. (Courtesy of Corps of Cadets, Texas A&M University)

the early campus and the Corps of Cadets, the "Keepers of the Spirit," whose daily formations gave the walk its name.[21]

Before leaving A&M to serve as the Secretary of Defense, president Gates had secured funds to hire 449 new faculty members, and focused attention on the need to develop the liberal arts, again placing pressure to provide new space and the rehabilitation of existing buildings.[22]

In 2007, the university commissioned the same professional team that produced the Campus Master Plan to develop a more detailed analysis of the center of the campus. The *Historic Core District Plan*[23] encouraged the development of Heritage Building Guidelines that drew heavily on the nationally used Secretary of the Interior's Standards for the Treatment of Historic Properties. It also proposed a new building to house Liberal Arts, Arts, and Humanities to be located at the west end of the East Quadrangle, responding to one of the Vision 2020 imperatives concerning the humanities.

Institutionalizing Planning and Design Decisions

To better coordinate recommendations on physical changes, the CBE was placed under the co-chairmanship of the provost and executive vice president, the chief academic officer of the university, and the vice president for finance and administration, ensuring that final decisions by the president of the university were based on input from the highest level.[24] The Design Review Board, chaired by the university architect, was re-established as a sub-council of the CBE, joining sub-councils for Facilities Utilization and Planning, Maintenance Review, and Technical Review, each of whose chairs provide expert advice to the CBE decision-making process. Comprehensive evaluation of changes to the physical environment of the campus, including care of its built heritage, had finally been institutionalized. In 2008, after a hiatus of over fifty years, the university appointed a university architect to provide day-to-day oversight of the Campus Master Plan's implementation and the design review sub-council.[25] Lilia Y. Gonzales '94, AIA, LEED AP, was appointed to this position in September 2012. The Office of University Architect expanded to include a campus planner and a project architect,

works across the university community to increase awareness of the value of good design, guide the development of new building projects, and oversee the reuse of heritage buildings following established preservation principles.

Applying New Policies, Procedures, and Principles

The YMCA Building

One of the first buildings in the Historic Core to be considered for re-use was the YMCA Building. Long superseded by the MSC as the social center of the campus, it had provided office space for a variety of service agencies including the university police and student services, until they also moved out in 2003, leaving the building vacant. Significantly, the request for professional qualifications asked for an architectural firm with historic preservation experience to lead the design team. Since the program of requirements for the YMCA re-use called for floor space far in excess of that available in the 1914 building, it was agreed that the east wing that contained the abandoned swimming pool and former chapel would be demolished, and a larger wing added to establish a "presence" on the Academic Plaza, and provide an accessible entry from Military Walk. Quimby McCoy Preservation Architecture, LLP, Dallas, were the architects, with Vaughn Construction as contractor for the project that was rededicated on November 8, 2012.

The Memorial Student Center

While the work to the YMCA Building created new academic space, the growth of the student body, from 36,675 in 1985 to nearly 45,000 twenty years later, had a significant impact on space for social and leadership purposes, referred to at A&M as "the other education." The MSC had been built in 1951 to serve fewer than 7,000 students, and was last expanded in the early 1980s. Working with student leaders and alumni, the university undertook a programming study in 2008 that called for a complete reorganization of much of the plan, and identified the need for a substantial addition. Perkins + Will, Architects,

The work to the YMCA Building followed National Park Service preservation principles for the treatment of historic buildings. The 1914–20 structure at the left in the photograph received some exterior restoration and interior rehabilitation that included removing dropped ceilings and interior walls to return the major entry space on the main floor to its former glory. The addition on the right is respectful of the original, using modified brick detailing at the corners and one-over-one windows on the upper floors, to differentiate old from new. The new "hyphen" between them is defined by its metal cladding, and contains vertical circulation and other functions that serve both sides of the building. (Photograph by Carolyn Brown, courtesy of Quimby McCoy Preservation Architecture, LLP.)

The 1952 Memorial Student Center, a Prairie Style building (shown on page 196), guided the design of the addition, even reopening the original stone quarry. The photograph shows the southeast entry into the Twelfth Man Hall, with the Rudder Tower to the right, and newly opened windows that face Kyle Field. (Photograph by Ian Muise)

recreated the MSC developing light-filled, vibrant interiors and added a 15,000-square-foot ballroom, new art galleries, and meeting rooms. Vaughn Construction was the contractor for the $94 million project. Like all campus projects, the MSC was designed to meet at least Leadership in Energy and Design (LEED) Silver standards.

The Corps Dormitories

The south-side dormitories designed by Albert Finn, and constructed in 1939, consisted of twelve simple double-loaded corridor buildings arranged to form a series of open spaces. They lacked many basic amenities expected even in military housing, and while single-story meeting spaces had been added at the corners of the original layout during the Rudder years, the complex lacked sufficient student meeting areas, offices for counseling and leadership groups, and general lounge areas appropriate to a Corps of Cadets that was expanding its ranks. The 1939 buildings

also had significant code, life-safety, and accessibility deficiencies. The Rudder-era additions were demolished to make way for full-height corner insertions that solved both programmatic and regulatory needs. Smith and Company, Architects followed the university's Heritage Building Guidelines in their design of the initial corner connection between two of the 1939 dormitory buildings, for which Vaughn Construction were contractors. The completion phase included the rest of the Corps Dorm complex, and was designed by Kirksey Architecture of Houston, with Spaw Glass Construction, Inc. as contractors.

Francis Hall

At Francis Hall, one of the oldest buildings on campus, the rehabilitation philosophy was more dramatic, but still in keeping with the campus guidelines. Built in 1918 to house the first veterinary hospital, supplanted in 1932 by Vosper's hospital, Francis Hall had been occupied by a variety of departments.

Smith Architects separated the old from the new by using the same two brick colors as the original, but reversed in terms of body and banding. The horizontals of the windows are continued, with a clear differentiation in the use of glass curtain walling. The new structure is connected to the old at the second and third levels, leaving a clear passage into the 1939 quadrangle at ground level. (Photograph by Ian Muise)

Much altered to meet academic needs, the original two-story surgical teaching room with its bleacher seating had been lost when a concrete floor was inserted to create a second floor lecture hall. In 2011, the building became vacant, and was assigned to the Department of Construction Science. Again, the university's primary concerns were code and life safety, but after a successful fund-raising campaign, and a thorough study of the programmatic needs, it was decided to restore the exterior of the

The 1918 interior of Francis Hall was stripped back to its reinforced concrete structure, and new glass walls were added, with exposed mechanical and lighting systems to serve as teaching tools. The original floor and wall patterns were marked by subtle changes in color, making the "ghosts" of the old readable in the new facility. (Photograph by Marcel Erminy)

building, provide easy access to the main entrance, and repair the original fabric. Interior walls were largely removed and the space remade to meet new teaching and research needs, using contemporary materials and details. Brown Reynolds Watford, Architects, Dallas office transformed one of the oldest buildings on campus by recovering the past and celebrating the future. The issue of accessibility was resolved by the sensitive stair/ramp combination on the main south façade, and a dramatic reworking of the first floor to allow access to a new elevator and other services. The architects took out the later concrete floor and recreated the two-story surgical teaching space as a large first floor classroom, reopening the 1918 skylight. Satterfield and Pontikes Construction, Inc. were the contractors.

Reworking Vosper's Buildings

As has been described in the earlier chapters, Vosper's buildings have also undergone changes over the years, based on the need to prepare for new users and meet evolving building standards. In the case of the 1932 Administration Building, now named for Jack K. Williams, the opportunity was taken to restore the intended function of the building as the Office of the President and senior campus administrators. In Scoates Hall, occupied since its inception by the Agricultural Engineering Department, now Biological and Agricultural Engineering, the design team was able to recreate some of Vosper's 1932 design intent, while transforming the agricultural machine shops to office and research space. At the Animal Industries Building, assignment of the building to the Department of Nuclear Engineering, combined with code and life-safety changes, had the potential for negative impact on Vosper's spatial organization and decorative finishes. In developing the work program, the university architect worked with the project architect and consultants to develop a simplified *Historic Structures Report*, a document that identifies significant historic features, significant interior spaces, and original finishes and details so that changes could be made with minimal impact. Such reports have now been incorporated into the standard procedures for working on heritage buildings on the campus.[26]

The Future

By the time the Center for Heritage Conservation (CHC) was created in 2005, there were already clear signs that the CHC mantra, "making the past a significant part of our future," had been accepted as university policy. The 2004 Campus Master Plan recommended that it be reviewed after ten years. In 2015, the university commissioned Ayers Saint Gross, Architects and Planners, to undertake a comprehensive review of the entire plan. The underlying goals and objectives included enhancement of the student experience, improvement to campus connectivity (both physical and academic), and an integrated vision for the campus landscape and its facilities.[27] The brief to the consulting team called for a specific section on historic preservation.[28] The draft report submitted in October 2016 identified "legacy or heritage assets," and proposes an integrated approach to preservation guidelines for the campus. In categorizing existing buildings by four levels of significance, specific reference was made to post-war era and Modern Movement buildings built between 1945 and 1965.[29] National studies have concluded that the significance of existing buildings should be considered on a continuous time frame, using criteria that respond to the original design intent, and perceived community value, and that the review process should be continuous, so that newer buildings are included automatically.[30]

In his letter to the Texas A&M family published in the 2004 Campus Master Plan, President Robert M. Gates noted that, "a university's excellence is, and always will be, measured first and foremost by the quality of its programs, students and faculty. Its built environment – from buildings and other structures to the space that surrounds and contains them – must be their equal. The quality of Texas A&M University's facilities must reflect the quality of the people and programs they house."[31]

The architecture of Vosper was rooted in the Beaux-Arts tradition that connected built form with such high ideals. Vosper's work is indeed an "architecture that speaks" to the essence of the A&M College of Texas. Beginning in the last two decades of the twentieth century, recognition of Vosper's legacy, and the legacy of the many other designers who have shaped the built environment of the campus, and in turn shaped its users, has taken its rightful place in the political will of the institution.

As the university moves forward, now exceeding an enrollment of 60,000 students, the challenge is to maintain a physical environment that not only "reflects the quality of the people and programs," but one that reflects leadership toward a future that is sustainable economically, environmentally, and culturally. Texas A&M University must be an institution that creates new buildings that serve their purpose well, minimize their impact on the environment, and have the flexibility to meet future needs, housed on a campus that shows loyalty to, and respect for, the architecture of the past, using it wisely and creatively. In short, a campus whose architecture matches the excellence, integrity, and delight that are manifest in the work of S. C. P. Vosper; educating, supporting and inspiring future generations.

Afterword

CREATING A SENSE OF PLACE

THIS BOOK describes the creation of the unique place that we know as Texas A&M University. The buildings and spaces with which we connect shape our memories. My recollections of daily walks from the Memorial Student Center to the Langford Architecture Building, and the connecting spaces in between, will forever be a part of my experiences at Texas A&M University, and I carry them with me in my role as university architect. In a university setting, it is collective memories such as mine that shape the traditions and legacies of the institution.

Since 2015, Texas A&M University has been working with consultants, Ayers Saint Gross, to update the 2004 Campus Master Plan. Taking cues from the civic structure defined by Frederick Giesecke and Frederick W. Hensel Jr., most recognizable in the current Historic Core of the campus, the update has focused on the creation of a network of open spaces (quadrangles, plazas, and green spaces), pedestrian malls, and connectors and links, that can unify the campus in both north-south and east-west orientations.

At the same time, the Campus Master Plan pays special attention to the historic fabric of the campus. This includes interior organization and decorative elements, as well as the exterior appearance of our rich heritage buildings, historic vistas, outdoor spaces, and pedestrian walkways such as Military Walk. The plan will provide guidelines to maintain the authenticity and uniqueness of place and spaces, while promoting sustainability through the adaptive reuse of existing buildings.

As the university continues to grow, the Campus Guidelines in the Campus Master Plan, will establish the values for the physical environment. These include supporting education, teaching, and research; respecting tradition and legacy; enhancing campus identity; connecting people and place; and improving the campus experience. These values will set the context for the development of principles to guide the architectural vocabulary of future buildings. This includes the articulation of building façades into elements, creating building entrances that articulate a building's character and identity ("architecture that speaks"), and building materiality.

The challenge for a campus as large and architecturally diverse as Texas A&M University is to create unity and identity through consistent, yet flexible, building design parameters based on campus "character zones" that reflect different geographical areas of the campus. We must respond to the challenge of changing teaching pedagogies, the incorporation of large collaborative spaces, and ever-changing technologies; each of which impact the form of our physical facilities and call for flexibility within clearly defined, value-driven parameters.

The Office of the University Architect is dedicated to an integrated approach to the long-term sustainability and management of architectural, environmental, cultural, and land resources of the Texas A&M University campus, while maintaining and creating a campus that, like the buildings designed by S. C. P. Vosper, continue to inspire and delight. The conservation of the heritage of buildings such as Vosper's is imperative to telling our architectural story and our proud campus history; *Architecture That Speaks: S. C. P. Vosper and Ten Remarkable Buildings at Texas A&M* is a part of the educational experience.

—Lilia Y. Gonzales, AIA, LEED AP
University Architect, Texas A&M University
December 2016

(Courtesy of Ayers Saint Gross Architects and Planners)

Appendix

VOSPER-DESIGNED BUILDINGS IN TEXAS

MUCH OF S. C. P. Vosper's work was accomplished within firms led by other architects and as a result, it is more difficult to document the buildings for which Vosper could be credited as the designer. The following list is compiled for buildings for which there is more than one source documenting Vosper's design role.

Eastern Star Home, Arlington, 1924 (for Herbert M. Greene Company, designer; Ralph H. Cameron, supervising architect); demolished

Scottish Rite Cathedral, San Antonio, 1924 (for Herbert M. Greene Company, designer; Ralph H. Cameron, supervising architect)

Medical Arts Building, San Antonio, 1926 (for Ralph H. Cameron)

Theodore Roosevelt Elementary School Addition, McAllen, 1927 (for Ralph H. Cameron); attribution to Vosper is inconclusive but the ornamental work at the entrance is exuberant and Vosper was working in Cameron's office at the time it was designed.

Central Christian Church, Austin, 1928 (for Ralph H. Cameron with Robert Leon White)

Grace Lutheran Church, San Antonio, 1928–29 (for Ralph H. Cameron)

Plan for the waterfront, City of Corpus Christi, 1928 (with Gutzon Borglum); it is unknown if this plan was executed and if Vosper collaborated with another architect for this work.

Monument in bronze for the Texas Memorial Stadium, University of Texas, Austin, 1929 (with Hugo Villa)

John Sealy Hospital plans for an addition, Galveston, c. 1929 (with Robert Leon White)

Chemistry Building, Texas A&M University, College Station, 1929–33 (for F. E. Giesecke, college architect)

Cushing Library, Texas A&M University, College Station, 1930 (for F. E. Giesecke, college architect)

Hart Hall, Texas A&M University, College Station, 1930 (for F. E. Giesecke, college architect)

Walton Hall, Texas A&M University, College Station, 1931 (for F. E. Giesecke, college architect)

Petroleum Engineering, Geology and Engineering Experiment Station Building, Texas A&M University, College Station, 1933 (for F. E. Giesecke, college architect)

Veterinary Hospital, Texas A&M University, College Station, 1933 (for F. E. Giesecke, college architect)

Administration Building, Texas A&M University, College Station, 1933 (for F. E. Giesecke, college architect)

Agricultural Engineering Building, Texas A&M University, College Station, 1933 (for F. E. Giesecke, college architect)

Animal Industries Building, Texas A&M University, College Station, 1934 (for F. E. Giesecke, college architect)

Longhorn Caverns State Park, Burnett, 1934–38 (for National Park Service); the Administration Building and most likely the custodian's dwelling are attributable to Vosper. Vosper's drawings for various cabins and custodian dwellings are very similar to the extant custodian's dwelling design. Vosper left the Burnett site for Goliad in 1935.

Goliad State Park Caretaker's Dwelling, Goliad, c. 1938 (for National Park Service; with Raiford L. Stripling)

Mission Nuestra Senora del Espiritu Santo de Zuniga, Goliad State Park, Goliad, 1935–41 (for National Park Service; with Raiford L. Stripling)

Goliad Memorial Auditorium, Goliad, 1936 (Vosper & Stripling Architects)

Fannin State Park, now Fannin Battleground State Historic Site, Goliad, c. 1937 (SCP Vosper and Raiford L. Stripling, Architects)

Fannin Memorial Monument, Goliad State Park, Goliad 1937, (Vosper & Stripling Architects for park; Donald Nelson architect with Raoul Josset, sculptor for monument)

Presidio Nuestra Senora de Loreto de la Bahia, Goliad, 1935–41 (early studies while working on the Mission Nuestra Senora del Espiritu Santo de Zuniga nearby for National Park Service; with Raiford Stripling)

Varisco Building, Bryan, 1948 (for Philip G. Norton)

A note on the building program at The University of Texas at Austin (UT), led by Herbert M. Greene as principal designer and Robert Leon White as Supervising Architect: No direct evidence was found of Vosper's work on any of the buildings completed under the 1922–30 building program except for the Women's Gymnasium, completed in 1931, for which Vosper prepared a rendering. That Vosper worked for Greene in Dallas and later began teaching at UT may be coincidental. Greene's drawings do not indicate who drew or traced them and White's papers did not yield record of a role for Vosper. Because Vosper was essentially commuting to Austin from San Antonio, where he had extensive work on the boards in Cameron's office during the same period, he may not have worked with White on the UT building program. However, further research should be undertaken to confirm the assumption made here that Vosper was not involved with these buildings by reviewing the drawings prepared under White's direction and other resources. The building program for the period of 1922–30 included the Texas Memorial Stadium (1924; for which Vosper produced a bronze panel with Hugo Villa in 1929 after leaving his teaching position), Biology Building (1925), Recitation Building (Garrison Hall; 1926), Wooldridge Hall (1924, demolished 2010), Littlefield Memorial Dormitory (Littlefield Residence Hall; 1927 or 1929), Gregory Gymnasium (1930), and Chemistry Building (Welch Hall; 1931). Not attributed to Greene is the Women's Gymnasium (later named for Anna Hiss; 1931, partially demolished), the only building of this period with a direct link to Vosper. The extent of his role on this project is unknown but his signature is found on a rendering of the building in the Alexander Architectural Archives at UT. Vosper is known to have prepared renderings for White for the Alamo National Bank Building in 1928 and may have been hired for the rendering exclusively.

Notes

CHAPTER 1

1. In developing the background for this examination of the work of Samuel Charles Phelps Vosper on the Texas A&M University campus, Henry C. Dethloff, *A Centennial History of Texas A&M University 1876–1976*, (College Station: Texas A&M University Press, 1975) remains the single most valuable reference on the establishment of the A&M College of Texas, and its transformation to a Tier One Research University by 1976.

2. Ibid., 5.

3. Ibid., 11–12.

4. Ibid., 14.

5. Margaret Lis van Bavel, *Birth and Death of Boonville* (Austin: Nortex Press, 1986), 93.

6. Dethloff, *Centennial History*, 18.

7. Ernest Langford, "Here We'll Build the College" (unpublished manuscript, Cushing Memorial Library and Archives, Texas A&M University, 1963, iii). After describing the siting of the college, Langford, who graduated from A&M in architectural engineering in 1913, and served as College Archivist from 1957–1971, follows with a chronological list of every major building constructed on the campus from 1875–1963, with a description and details on designers, contractors, and cost. Langford also offers his own observations on selected buildings.

8. From the Foreword to Dethloff's *Centennial History*, xii.

9. Ibid., 6–14.

10. Texas State History Handbook Online, accessed March 2, 2016, https://tshaonline.org/handbook/online.

11. Langford, "Here We'll Build the College," 11.

12. David Brooks Cofer, *Early History of Texas A&M College Through Letters and Papers* (College Station: Texas A&M University Press, 1952) quoted in Glenna Fourman Brundidge, Paul David McKay, and Paul Robert Scott, eds., *Brazos County History: Rich Past-Bright Future*, (Bryan, TX: Family History Foundation, 1986), 420.

13. F. E. Giesecke's unpublished 15-page autobiography was sent to D. B. Cofer, then the college archivist, by letters dated June 20 and June 23, 1953. The second letter was written just hours before Giesecke was stricken by a fatal heart attack.

14. All references to the names of buildings, dates of their construction, and names of designers are taken from Ernest Langford's "Here We'll Build the College."

15. Langford, "Here We'll Build the College," 41.

16. Ibid. Langford's research as university archivist developed a detailed chronology of every campus building from 1875 to 1963.

17. Giesecke, autobiography, 5.

18. The Experiment Station Building housed the Texas Agricultural Extension Service; The Civil Engineering Building, later named for James C. Nagle; Legett, Milner and Mitchell were residence halls; The Electrical Engineering Building, later named Bolton Hall; the Mess Hall, later named for Bernard Sbisa; and the Academic Building.

19. Obituary, *Summer Texan*, Sunday, August 19, 1945, Samuel Gideon Papers, 1908–1945, Center for American History, The University of Texas at Austin.

20. Giesecke, autobiography, 7.

21. Dethloff, *Centennial History*, 230.

22. Giesecke, autobiography, 7.

23. John Knox Walker, *Over At College: A Texas A&M Kid in the 1930s* (College Station: Texas A&M University Press, 2016). Walker's personal reminiscence provides an extraordinary insight into life on the campus during the Depression years.

24. Dethloff, *Centennial History*, 415–420, covers the negotiations with the University of Texas and the Texas State Legislature that *culminated* in the passage of the bill on April 8, 1931, that provided a final settlement of the distribution of the Permanent University Fund.

25. Giesecke, autobiography, 10.

26. Brundidge, McKay, and Scott, *Brazos County History*, 421.

27. Dethloff, *Centennial History*, 424.

CHAPTER 2

1. Notes from letter from T. U. Taylor, Acting Chairman and Dean of the College of Engineering, to W. S. Sutton, Interim President, dated August 8, 1923, attached to which is a "Statement of Training and Experience of S. C. P. Vosper," transcribed by Lila Knight. This document is believed to be located in the Briscoe Center for American History but was not located by the author. Knight wrote a history of the University of Texas architecture department and shared notes from her research via email on multiple occasions. Knight is also the author of Vosper's entry in the *Handbook of Texas Online* and of an article on Vosper's work in *Texas Architect* magazine.

2. *Year Book of the Architectural League of New York* (New York: Press of the Kalkhoff Company, 1914), 128. This year book identifies Vosper as a student of Columbia University. Contacting Columbia University for verification of Vosper as a student of the college yielded no records; records of students that were members of an atelier were not available.

3. "Long, Birch Bernadette (1878–1927)," Philadelphia Architects and Buildings, accessed June 25, 2016, https://www.philadelphiabuildings.org/pab/app/ar_display.cfm/150608. Biography from the *American Architects and Buildings* database.

4. Michael McCullar, *Restoring Texas, Raiford Stripling's Life and Architecture* (College Station: Texas A&M Press, 1985), 32. This book is the best single source of information on Vosper's life, with anecdotal stories derived from interviews with Stripling and Vosper's son Bradley, as well as other colleagues of Vosper and Stripling.

5. Ibid., 33.

6. Notes transcribed by Lila Knight.

7. "Acts to Dissolve Big Lasky Concern as 'Movie Trust,'" *New York World*, accessed November 27, 2016, http://www.cobbles.com/simpp_archive/ftc-case_1921.htm.

8. Katy Capt, "Raiford Leak Stripling: Starving to Death on My Own Terms (unpublished study, 1981), 29. This study was prepared based significantly on taped interviews with Raiford Stripling in 1981 and contains many anecdotal quotes by Stripling about Vosper.

9. Copy of a handwritten resolution from F. E. Giesecke, undated but annotated as "April 1924," Alexander Architectural Archives, University of Texas at Austin, School of Architecture Faculty notebook, compiled by Lila Knight, which includes copies of correspondence collected by Knight from other sources, principally the Briscoe Center for American History.

10. "Scottish Rite Soon to Lay Cornerstone of Million-Dollar Cathedral Building," *San Antonio Express*, October 1, 1922.

11. Notes from letter from T. U. Taylor, transcribed by Lila Knight.

12. McCullar, *Restoring Texas*, 33.

13. Ibid. .

14. Dean of Engineering T. U. Taylor, letter to President H. Y. Benedict, April 3, 1928, in the Alexander Architectural Archives, University of Texas at Austin.

15. Robert Leon White, letter to President H. Y. Benedict, May 25, 1928, in the Alexander Architectural Archives, University of Texas at Austin.

16. "Vosper Is Added to Teaching Staff of A&M College," *The Bryan Daily Eagle*, September 10, 1927, and "Dr. F. E. Giesecke, Former A&M Student and Later Faculty Member at Texas, to Be Architectural Head," *The Bryan Daily Eagle*, September 23, 1927.

17. *Austin American Statesman*, November 8, 1928, 2.

18. McCullar, *Restoring Texas*, 33.

19. Ernest Langford, *The First Fifty Years of Architectural Education at the Agricultural and Mechanical College of Texas* (College Station: Library Archives, 1957), 9. A *projet* is the French term for an architectural problem.

20. Capt, "Raiford Leak Stripling," 13.

21. McCullar, *Restoring Texas*, 38.

22. Ibid, 13.

23. James Knox Walker Jr., *Over at College* (College Station: Texas A&M University Press, 2016), 78.

24. Cynthia Brandimarte and Angela Reed, *Texas State Parks and the CCC*, (College Station: Texas A&M University Press, 2013), 15.

25. Capt, "Raiford Leak Stripling," 29.

26. Brandimarte and Reed, *Texas State Parks and the CCC*, 27.

27. Capt, "Raiford Leak Stripling," 31.

CHAPTER 3

1. The dates for the use of this style vary with some historians suggesting 1930 as the cut-off date; one well-established style guide is *Identifying American Architecture* by Johan J. G. Blumeson, 1981.

2. For more information on the City Beautiful Movement, refer to publications by William H. Wilson, including *The City Beautiful Movement*, Baltimore: John Hopkins University Press, 1994.

3. The description of styles is reserved for other publications as there are many style guides and architectural historian's descriptions of their characteristics. The terms used in this book are consistent with the terms recommended by the US Department of the Interior, National Park Service guidelines for nominations to the National Register of Historic Places. More information can be found at https://www.nps.gov/nr/publications/guidance.htm.

CHAPTER 4

1. Stephen Hawking, interview by Ronald G. Carter, April 27, 1995, College Station, TX, and notes provided June 16, 2016. Carter has served as building proctor for more than forty years. This continuity, which is also a factor for Scoates Hall and until recently the Animal Industries Building, has resulted in buildings that are better cared for in general, as well as better preserved and appreciated.

2. Contract between A&M College and Welch and Company of Houston for interior painting at the Chemistry Building. July 25, 1952. A similar contract was executed for the Agricultural Engineering, Petroleum Engineering and the Cottonseed Laboratory Buildings, dated August 21, 1952, and for the Animal Industries Building.

3. Ronald Carter is the chair of the university's Classroom Improvement Committee, which starting in 2013 has helped to preserve the Vosper-designed lecture rooms while modernizing and making them more functional for students and faculty.

CHAPTER 5

1. "A&M College Needs New Library Building," *The Bryan Daily Eagle*, November 24, 1924.

2. David Chapman (retired university archivist), interview by Nancy McCoy, April 16, 2016, College Station, TX.

3. Jerry C. Cooper and Henry C. Dethloff, *Footsteps* (College Station: Texas A&M University Press, 1991), 161.

4. Mrs. Robert K. Fletcher (head cataloguer), "The Cushing Library of the Agricultural and Mechanical College of Texas," notes compiled for an oral presentation at a staff meeting, undated (but annotated "after 1944"), Cushing Memorial Library and Archives, College Station, 4.

5. Ibid.

6. Jhonny Langer (conservator and restoration artist), interview by Nancy McCoy, June 22, 2016, Dallas, TX. Langer was a partner in the restoration painting company of Local Color that was contracted to do the decorative painting for the restoration of Cushing Library. The firm and the students that assisted with the restoration discretely left their signatures in gold in one of the shields that are part of the ceiling decoration.

7. Fletcher, 2.

CHAPTER 6

1. "Welcome Fish!!! What Any Freshman Coming to Hart Needs to Know . . . ," last modified May 21, 2000, printed June 21, 2000, http://mothra.tamu.edu/halls/hart/fish_info.htm, and found in Cushing Library's clippings file.

2. "Two Hart Hall Men's Inconvenience 'Fun but Weird,'" *The Battalion*, January 24, 1978.

3. "Welcome Fish!!!"

4. Ibid.

5. "Walton 'Hotel' Provides Luxurious Comfort for 'Hard Working' Aggies," *The Battalion*, September 3, 1931.

CHAPTER 7

1. "Architect revitalizes old buildings," *The Bryan Eagle*, September 18, 1986. Calhoun is referring to an article in the *Texas Aggie* that used the term "architectural savagery."

2. "On Solid Ground, A&M Alumnus Halbouty Continues Life of Contributions to Geosciences," *The Battalion*, July 27, 1994.

3. Dr. Christopher C. Mathewson, PE, interview by Nancy McCoy, April 27, 2016, College Station, TX. Dr. Mathewson served as facility engineer/user coordinator and building proctor from 1980 to 2006. He shared the entirety of his digital file collection and recollections of his time in the building, which began in1981, during the April 27, 2016, interview and on other occasions. Dr. Mathewson, like other long-time building proctors, took a very personal and dedicated interest in the well-being of the building and its occupants during his tenure and is proud to have been part of its preservation as well as the improvements and changes that occurred, including his role as user coordinator for the addition. He noted that he has been complimented numerous times by former students and visitors for the preservation of the building and its historically significant features.

4. "Halbouty Building to Receive $3.6 Million Renovation Job," *The Battalion*, December 6, 1985.

5. "Landmark Coming Down," *The Pictorial Press*, August 3, 1972.

6. Ernest Langford, "Here We'll Build the College" (unpublished manuscript, July 1, 1963), 150–51.

7. "Landmark Coming Down." The connection between the colorful tiles of the tower dome and Mexican architecture, specifically the sixteenth- to eighteenth-century churches of the Puebla region is intriguing. Carolyn Brown photographically documented these churches in the 1990s, observing the elaborate use of color and decoration in the tile and plaster that decorates the entrances and domes of these buildings.

8. James L. Keith, letter to David Chapman (chief archivist, Cushing Memorial Library), May 27, 1999.

9. Ernest Langford, "Here We'll Build the College" (unpublished manuscript, July 1, 1963), 150.

CHAPTER 8

1. "Carved Stone Figures to Stay on Civil Engineering Building," *The Battalion*, February 15, 1984.

2. *Handbook of Texas Online*, Tamara Miner Haygood, "Texas Fever," accessed November 12, 2016, http://www.tshaonline.org/handbook/online/articles/awt01.

3. "History," accessed June 10, 2016, http://vetmed.tamu.edu/about-us/history.

4. *San Antonio Light*, August 21, 1946, 13.

5. James L. Keith, Jr., letter to David Chapman (chief archivist, Cushing Memorial Library), May 27, 1999.

6. *San Antonio Express*, November 8, 1948, p. 12. Vosper either returned for the funeral or had just returned to live in San Antonio after leaving Washington, DC.

7. "Carved stone figures to stay on civil engineering building."

CHAPTER 9

1. Ernest Langford, "Here We'll Build a College" (unpublished manuscript, July 1, 1963), 146–47.

2. "A New Administration Building Presents Convenient Floor Space; College Executives Office Moved," *The Battalion*, October 11, 1933, 1.

3. From the bidding and construction records donated by Fretz Construction to the Cushing Memorial Library and Archives. E. A. Fretz led the Standard Construction Company, and his grandson, Robert R. Fretz, Jr., is the president of Fretz Construction Company and is a Fellow of the Texas A&M University Center for Heritage Conservation, where he is active in helping support the preservation of this and other buildings.

4. "A&M renames building to honor former president," *The Battalion*, October 6, 1997.

5. Katy Capt, "Raiford Leak Stripling: Starving to Death on My Own Terms," (unpublished study, 1981), 14.

6. Lisa Nixon, "Buildings Worth Remembering," *The Texas Aggie* (May 1981), 7–10. This short article is a good summation of this entire book. Ms. Nixon had figured out the importance of this collection of buildings to the campus in 1981, the same year both she and the author graduated from A&M. Ironically, the author was not aware of, or does not remember Ms. Nixon or the article.

7. Melba Marini Champion, letter to Cushing Memorial Library, April 5, 1983. Ms. Champion, of Willis, Texas was a sculptor who upon visiting the campus near the fiftieth anniversary of the completion of the building, wrote about her thoughts and recollections and then sent them to the library.

CHAPTER 10

1. Matthew J. Mosca, historic paint finishes specialist who prepared a study of the finishes for this building in 2013. Mosca later prepared a similar study for the Petroleum Engineering and Geology Building in 2016. Mosca is one of the foremost experts in the United States on historic painted finishes.

2. Henry C. Dethloff and Stephen W. Searcy, *Engineering Agriculture at Texas A&M* (College Station: Texas A&M University Press, 2015), 40. The author wishes to acknowledge Dr. Searcy and BAEN for sharing historical information and photographs, some of which were collected for this book, written as part of the department's centennial celebration.

3. Board of Directors Meeting Minutes, special session, April 2, 1932, Texas A&M University, College Station.

4. "Scoates Hall Designated Historic Landmark," *The Texas Aggie* (July 1978).

5. Dr. Stephen W. Searcy, interview by Nancy McCoy, March 11, 2016, College Station, TX.

6. Bill Teeter, "Man Preserves Farming History with Antique Tractor Collection," *Waco Tribune*, October 18, 2010.

7. Lila Knight, research notes compiled and transmitted to the author on May 29, 2016.

8. Kurt Voss, interview by , 2013, May, and June 17, 2016, San Antonio, TX.

CHAPTER 11

1. Barron Rector, assistant professor, recounting a visit by one of the architects, named Harrison, who worked with Vosper, *The Battalion*, October 1, 1998.

CHAPTER 12

1. A history of campus houses was compiled by the late Professor Paul van Riper. It shows the location and occupants of most homes occupied in 1939, before the board of director's resolution to require their removal by 1941. The study was expanded by Justin Curtsinger, AIA '06, while he was a graduate assistant in the Center for Heritage Conservation. The materials are housed in the Cushing Memorial Library and Archives at Texas A&M University.

2. Robert Borden, *Historic Brazos County: An Illustrated History*, (Bryan, TX: Brazos Heritage Society, 2005), 71.

3. Glenn Fourman Brundidge, ed., *Brazos County History: Rich Past-Bright Future*, (Bryan, TX: Family History Foundation, 1986), 36.

4. Henry C. Dethloff, *A Centennial History of Texas A&M University 1876–1976*, (College Station: Texas A&M University Press, 1975), 456.

5. Frederick Ernst Giesecke (unpublished autobiography, 1953), Cushing Memorial Library and Archives, Texas A&M University, 14.

6. Dethloff, *A Centennial History*, 491.

7. Ernest Langford, "Here We'll Build the College," (unpublished manuscript, Cushing Memorial Library and Archives, Texas A&M University, 1963, 177).

8. Dethloff, *A Centennial History*, 556.

9. Ibid., 558.

10. Ibid., 562.

11. Ibid., 572.

12. Caudill Rowlett Scott, *Preliminary Campus Master Plan and Environmental Guidelines*, (College Station: Texas A&M University, March 1970.)

13. Dr. David Chapman (former Archivist, Texas A&M University), interview by Nancy McCoy and David Woodcock, April 15, 2016, Bryan, TX.

14. Winston S. Churchill, October 28, 1944, concerning the rebuilding of the House of Commons after a World War II bombing, noting that the shape of the room and the seating arrangement for its occupants influenced the nature of parliamentary debate.

15. Tim Donathen, AIA, interview by David Woodcock, April 12, 2016; Dr. Jerry Gaston, interview by, April 22, 2016. Both provided significant background data on physical planning policy in the three decades after 1985.

16. Donathen, then an architect with the Physical Plant Division, and Gaston, Head of Sociology at the time, provided insight into the restoration work to the Academic Building.

17. "Imperative 8," in *VISION 2020: Creating a Culture of Excellence*, (College Station: Texas A&M University, 1999), 52.

18. *Campus Master Plan, Texas A&M University*, (College Station: Texas A&M University, July 2004), 196.

19. Ibid.

20. Ibid., 17. Diagram of the Campus Civic Structure, from a draft of "The Campus Remembered" study, 2002, David Woodcock.

21. The donor who made the restoration possible, Dan A. Hughes '52, asked that the eight markers not only recall the buildings that flanked Military Walk, some no longer extant, but should also inspire those who travel along it with the lifelong values that are the core of an education at Texas A&M University.

22. Chuck Sippial (former vice president for facilities), interview by David Woodcock, April 8, 2016; Dr. William Perry (former Associate Provost), interview by David Woodcock, May 19, 2016. These interviews gave much invaluable information about decisions made during their time at Texas A&M University.

23. Barnes, Gromatsky, Kosarek Architects with Michael Dennis & Associates produced the *Historic Core District Plan* in December 2007.

24. Karan Watson, provost and executive vice president, was instrumental in reshaping the Council for the Built Environment (CBE), ensuring that each of the technical and design sub-councils would have a place at the table. Rodney McClendon, then vice president for administration, the other CBE co-chair, supported the appointment of a University Architect that had been recommended in the 2004 Campus Master Plan. Jerry Strawser, the current VP for Finance and Administration and co-chair of the CBE, continues this support.

25. David Godbey, AIA, had been a long-time professional in the Facilities Office of the university when he was appointed as interim university architect in 2008. He developed a checklist based on the recommendations of the Campus Master Plan to assist architects and the design review process, and worked on the initial design reviews for the building to be located in the East Quadrangle. In September 2012, Lilia Y. Gonzales' 94, AIA, LEED AP, assumed the university architect position, having served as architect to the University of North Texas System and with extensive experience in private practice.

26. Lilia Gonzales, interview by David Woodcock, March 15, 2016. Gonzales provided significant material on the development of institutional processes for the initiation and implementation of changes to the campus environment at Texas A&M University.

27. Lilia Gonzales, university architect, e-mail message to Texas A&M University faculty, students, and staff, October 10, 2016.

28. Ayers Saint Gross and their consultants followed a process similar to that for the 2004 Campus Master Plan, with a steering committee co-chaired by Jorge Vanegas, dean of the College of Architecture and Lilia Gonzales, university architect, and utilizing a series of focus groups. The six major components of the report include plans for campus development, mobility and safety, sustainability and wellness, conservation and heritage, wayfinding and signage, and campus guidelines (for building design and landscape.) The final Campus Master Plan Update is anticipated in December 2016.

29. The historic preservation consultants for the Campus Master Plan Review, Quimby McCoy Preservation Architecture, LLP, proposed four levels of significance for buildings fifty years old and older. The highest level, Level One, is Heritage Buildings, buildings that should be preserved and protected. The next levels, Historic Buildings and Secondary Buildings, call for the application of Heritage Guidelines as a baseline for change, but with broader application. The fourth level, Non-Contributing Buildings, uses National Register of Historic Places terminology to describe buildings that have useful purpose, but do not conform to the general appearance of the campus. The suggested historic preservation process calls for buildings to be evaluated automatically as they reach fifty years of age, and also whenever any building is being considered for major work program.

30. *Architecture for the Great Society: Strategies for Evaluation and Stewardship. The GSA Portfolio of Buildings Constructed during the 1960s and 1970s*, (Washington, DC: US General Services Administration, February 22, 2001), 19.

31. *Campus Master Plan*, v.

Bibliography

Alexander Architectural Archives, The University of Texas Libraries, The University of Texas at Austin, School of Architecture Faculty notebook, compiled by Lila Knight, former archivist.

Barnes Gromatsky Kosarek Architects, Michael Dennis and Associates, Dr. Bryce Jordan, Sasaki Associates, Paulien and Associates, Inc. *Campus Master Plan for Texas A&M University*. College Station, 2004.

Borden, Robert. *Historic Brazos County: An Illustrated History*. San Antonio: Brazos Heritage Society, 2005.

Brandimarte, Cynthia, and Angela Reed. *Texas State Parks and the CCC*. College Station: Texas A&M University Press, 2013.

Brundidge, Glenna Fourman, ed. *Brazos County History: Rich Past-Bright Future*. Bryan, TX: Family History Foundation, 1986.

Capt, Katy. "Raiford Leak Stripling: Starving to Death on My Own Terms." Unpublished study, 1981.

Cofer, David Brooks. *Early History of Texas A&M College Through Letters and Papers*. College Station: Texas A&M University Press, 1952.

Cooper, Jerry C., and Henry C Dethloff. *Footsteps*. College Station: Texas A&M University Press, 1991.

Dethloff, Henry C. *A Centennial History of Texas A&M University 1876–1976*. College Station: Texas A&M University Press, 1975.

Dethloff, Henry C., and Stephen W. Searcy. *Engineering Agriculture at Texas A&M, the First Hundred Years*. College Station: Texas A&M University Press, 2015.

Drexler, Arthur, ed. *The Architecture of the Ecole des Beaux-Arts*. New York: The Museum of Modern Art, 1977.

Fletcher, Mrs. Robert K. "The Cushing Library of the Agricultural and Mechanical College of Texas." Unpublished notes, College Station, TX: Cushing Memorial Library and Archives, 1944.

Fox, Stephen. "Bryan, College Station, A&M, An Architectural Tour." Special insert, *Cite The Architecture and Design Review of Houston* 41, (Spring 1998).

Giesecke, Frederick Ernst. Unpublished autobiography. Cushing Memorial Library and Archives, College Station: Texas A&M University, 1953.

Harris, Cyril M., ed. *Historic Architecture Sourcebook*. New York: McGraw-Hill, 1977.

Harwood, Buie. *Decorating Texas: Decorative Painting in the Lone Star State from 1850's to the 1950's*. Fort Worth: Texas Christian University Press, 1993.

Langford, Ernest. *The First Fifty Years of Architectural Education at the Agricultural and Mechanical College of Texas*. College Station: Cushing Memorial Library Archives, Texas A&M University, 1957.

Langford, Ernest. "Here We'll Build the College." Unpublished manuscript, College Station: Cushing Memorial Library and Archives, Texas A&M University, 1963.

Long, Birch Burdette. "The Use of Color in Architecture." *Brickbuilder* 23 (1914): 125–129.

McCullar, Michael. *Restoring Texas, Raiford Stripling's Life and Architecture*. College Station: Texas A&M University Press, 1985.

Nixon, Lisa. "Buildings Worth Remembering." *The Texas Aggie* (May 1981): 7–11.

Scully, Vincent. *American Architecture and Urbanism*. New York: Henry Holt and Company, 1988.

Stripling, Raiford L., Papers and drawings. Cushing Memorial Library and Archives, Texas A&M University.

US General Services Administration. Architecture for the Great Society: Strategies for Evaluation and Stewardship. The GSA Portfolio of Buildings Constructed during the 1960s and 1970s. Washington, DC: 2001.

van Bavel, Margaret Lis. *Birth and Death of Boonville*. Austin, TX: Nortex Press, 1986.

Walker, James Knox, Jr. *Over at College, A Texas A&M Campus Kid in the 1930's*. College Station: Texas A&M University Press, 2016.

Welch, Frank D. *On Becoming an Architect, a Memoir*. Fort Worth, TX: TCU Press, 2014.

Wilson, William H. *The City Beautiful Movement*. Baltimore, MD: Johns Hopkins University Press, 1994.

ARCHIVES AND REPOSITORIES

Cushing Memorial Library and Archives, Texas A&M University, College Station.

Dolph Briscoe Center for American History Collections. The University of Texas at Austin.

Greene LaRoche and Dahl Collection, Drawings, 1902–1953, the Alexander Architectural Archives, University of Texas Libraries, The University of Texas at Austin. Includes the Herbert M. Greene Company.

Ralph Cameron (1892–1970) Drawings and Architectural Records (1914–1970), San Antonio, South and Central Texas, Alexander Architectural Archives, University of Texas Libraries, The University of Texas at Austin.

Raiford L. Stripling Collection (1910–1990) Drawings and papers in College Station, Cushing Memorial Library and Archives, Texas A&M University.

Robert Leon White (1898–1964) Drawings, 1920–1928, Mission San Jose, San Antonio and projects in Austin, Texas, Alexander Architectural Archives, University of Texas Libraries, The University of Texas at Austin.

Sam Houston Sanders Corps of Cadets Center. Archive, Texas A&M University.

San Antonio Conservation Society. Library.

Texas Parks and Wildlife Department records.

Texas State Library and Archives Commission. Archives and Information Services Division.

RELEVANT WEB SITES

American Institute of Architects. "The AIA Historical Directory of American Architects." http://public.aia.org/sites/hdoaa/wiki/Wiki%20 Pages/What's%20here.aspx.

Cushing Memorial Library and Archives, Texas A&M University, "Historic Images of Texas A&M University." https://www.flickr.com/ photos/cushinglibrary/collections/72157616848695613/.

Simon, Madlen. "The Beaux-Arts Atelier in America." Paper presented at the 84th Annual Meeting and Technology Conference of the Association of Collegiate Schools of Architecture, http://apps.acsa-arch .org/resources/proceedings/indexsearch.aspx?txtKeyword1=%22 Simon%2C+Madlen%22&ddField1=1.

Texas A&M University, College of Architecture. "History." http://www .arch.tamu.edu/inside/history/.

Texas Parks and Wildlife Department. "Civilian Conservation Corps Legacy Parks." http://tpwd.texas.gov/spdest/findadest/historic_sites/ ccc/.

Texas Parks and Wildlife Department. "The Look of Nature, Designing Texas State Parks During the Great Depression." http://texascccparks .org/parks/.

Texas State Historical Association. "The Handbook of Texas Online." https://tshaonline.org/handbook/online.

Texas State Library and Archives Commission. "Texas Parks Civilian Conservation Corps Drawing Database." https://www.tsl.texas.gov/ apps/arc/CCCDrawings.

Index